BAZI STRUCTURES

&

Structural Useful Gods

EARTH 土

戊 Wu
己 Ji

BaZi Structures & Structural Useful Gods
Earth Structure

The author can be reached at:

Mastery Academy of Chinese Metaphysics Sdn. Bhd. (611143-A)
19-3, The Boulevard, Mid Valley City,
59200 Kuala Lumpur, Malaysia.
Tel   : +603-2284 8080
Fax   : +603-2284 1218
Email   : info@masteryacademy.com
Website: www.masteryacademy.com

DISCLAIMER:

The author, Joey Yap and the publisher, JY Books Sdn Bhd, have made their best efforts to produce this high quality, informative and helpful book. They have verified the technical accuracy of the information and contents of this book. Any information pertaining to the events, occurrences, dates and other details relating to the person or persons, dead or alive, and to the companies have been verified to the best of their abilities based on information obtained or extracted from various websites, newspaper clippings and other public media. However, they make no representation or warranties of any kind with regard to the contents of this book and accept no liability of any kind for any losses or damages caused or alleged to be caused directly or indirectly from using the information contained herein.

Published by JY Books Sdn. Bhd. (659134-T)

Table of Contents

Wu 戊 Earth Day Master, Born in :

Table of Contents

About The Chinese Metaphysics Reference Series

Reference Series

The Chinese Metaphysics Reference Series of books are designed primarily to be used as complimentary textbooks for scholars, students, researchers, teachers and practitioners of Chinese Metaphysics.

The goal is to provide quick easy reference tables, diagrams and charts, facilitating the study and practice of various Chinese Metaphysics subjects including Feng Shui, BaZi, Yi Jing, Zi Wei, Liu Ren, Ze Ri, Ta Yi, Qi Men and Mian Xiang.

This series of books are intended as <u>reference text and educational materials</u> principally for the academic syllabuses of the **Mastery Academy of Chinese Metaphysics**. The contents have also been formatted so that Feng Shui Masters and other teachers of Chinese Metaphysics will always have a definitive source of reference at hand, when teaching or applying their art.

Because each school of Chinese Metaphysics is different, the Reference Series of books usually do not contain any specific commentaries, application methods or explanations on the theory behind the formulas presented in its contents. This is to ensure that the contents can be used freely and independently by all Feng Shui Masters and teachers of Chinese Metaphysics without conflict.

If you would like to study or learn the applications of any of the formulas presented in the Reference Series of books, we recommend that you undertake the courses offered by Joey Yap and his team of Instructors at the Mastery Academy of Chinese Metaphysics.

Titles offers in the Reference Series:

1. The Chinese Metaphysics Compendium
2. Dong Gong Date Selection
3. Earth Study Discern Truth
4. Xuan Kong Da Gua Structure Reference Book
5. San Yuan Dragon Gate Eight Formations Water Method
6. Xuan Kong Da Gua Ten Thousand Year Calendar
7. Plum Blossom Divination Reference Book
8. The Date Selection Compendium (Book 1) - The 60 Jia Zi Attributes
9. BaZi Structures & Structural Useful Gods Reference Series

Preface

The study and practice of BaZi is an infinitely rewarding and intriguing one, with literally an inexhaustible depth and range from which we can mine our information on a person's character, temperament, life outlook and personal destiny. The simplest data – your birth date and time – can yield a rich treasure trove of knowledge, most of which can help shed new light on old perceptions.

The idea for this BaZi Structures and Structural Useful God Reference Series came out of a common need among my BaZi students, many of whom wanted to learn more about how the various structures in BaZi are derived. This series was therefore created to help students learn and absorb the methods and techniques in which a structure is created and developed mainly from a classical standpoint.

While initially it was my idea to create one BaZi Structures book to accommodate all 10 Heavenly Stems (Day Masters), I soon found out that it would not be a book that could reasonably be used by anyone – because it would be too heavy to lift! So I decided to break it apart into five different books, with each one corresponding to each Element. The book you're holding in your hands is on Metal Structures, for both Wu 戊 and Ji 己 Earth Day Masters.

There are many traditional sources available on the BaZi structures, and the derivation of those structures. One of the more well-known texts is the *Qiong Tong Bao Jian* 窮通寶鑑, written by a famous master, *Xu Le Wu* 徐樂吾. Another popular BaZi scholar of recent past who contributed a lot to mainstream BaZi theories, especially those relating to structures, is *Wei Qian Li* 韋千里.

It's difficult for most students to have access to this information because it's scattered about in various texts and documents, and also – all of it is available only in Chinese. It was my intention, therefore, to compile this information into one convenient source, and to present the transliterated version of these traditional texts for the modern, English-speaking practitioner and student without losing the essence of the original.

To derive a structure and structural Useful God in BaZi, one must know and understand the Day Master and the month of birth, and its variations in a BaZi chart. There are traditional methods on how this is derived, and there are newer interpretations on these methods.

As such, different practitioners and teachers have different methods and formats to derive these structures, and it is recommended that you use the techniques outlined in this book with care and thought. As always, there is much merit in using traditional practices, but students who are learning BaZi should use this under the supervision of a teacher in order to better understand the subject. A good teacher will help you understand the different ways of interpreting these traditional texts.

Do note that these texts should not be taken literally. Different masters may agree or disagree with the classical commentaries included here, and as a student, it's important for you to know the reasons why. Better yet, it's important for you to know those reasons and then go on to form your own conclusions, based on your understanding of the various interpretations.

For that reason, this book was designed to be a reference accompaniment for the students of my BaZi Mastery Series, where you'll be able to get the guidance you need in interpreting these traditional methods. I encourage you to take a class because it will help to place this material in context and give you the added knowledge you need to help you make the most of the information contained within this book. Each and every structure in this book could be its own chapter, because it can literally explain a person and his or her modus operandi!

I hope you enjoy your research on this subject, and here's to many pleasurable hours of BaZi Structural study!

Warm regards,

Joey Yap
July 2009

Author's personal websites :
www.joeyyap.com I www.fengshuilogy.com (Personal blog)

Academy websites :
www.masteryacademy.com I www.masteryjournal.com I www.maelearning.com

Follow Joey's current updates on Twitter :
www.twitter.com/joeyyap

MASTERY ACADEMY
OF CHINESE METAPHYSICS™

At **www.masteryacademy.com**, you will find some useful tools to ascertain key information about the Feng Shui of a property or for the study of Astrology.

The Joey Yap Flying Stars Calculator can be utilised to plot your home or office Flying Stars chart. To find out your personal best directions, use the 8 Mansions Calculator. To learn more about your personal Destiny, you can use the Joey Yap BaZi Ming Pan Calculator to plot your Four Pillars of Destiny – you just need to have your date of birth (day, month, year) and time of birth.

For more information about BaZi, Xuan Kong or Flying Star Feng Shui, or if you wish to learn more about these subjects with Joey Yap, logon to the Mastery Academy of Chinese Metaphysics website at **www.masteryacademy.com.**

MASTERY ACADEMY
E-LEARNING CENTER
www.maelearning.com

www.maelearning.com

Bookmark this address on your computer, and visit this newly-launched website today. With the E-Learning Center, knowledge of Chinese Metaphysics is a mere 'click' away!

Our E-Learning Center consists of 3 distinct components.

1. Online Courses
These shall comprise of 3 Programs: our Online Feng Shui Program, Online BaZi Program, and Online Mian Xiang Program. Each lesson contains a video lecture, slide presentation and downloadable course notes.

2. MA Live!
With MA Live!, Joey Yap's workshops, tutorials, courses and seminars on various Chinese Metaphysics subjects broadcasted right to your computer screen. Better still, participants will not only get to see and hear Joey talk 'live', but also get to engage themselves directly in the event and more importantly, TALK to Joey via the MA Live! interface. All the benefits of a live class, minus the hassle of actually having to attend one!

3. Video-On-Demand (VOD)
Get immediate streaming-downloads of the Mastery Academy's wide range of educational DVDs, right on your computer screen. No more shipping costs and waiting time to be incurred!

Study at your own pace, and interact with your Instructor and fellow students worldwide… at your own convenience and privacy. With our E-Learning Center, knowledge of Chinese Metaphysics is brought DIRECTLY to you in all its clarity, with illustrated presentations and comprehensive notes expediting your learning curve!

Welcome to the Mastery Academy's E-LEARNING CENTER…YOUR virtual gateway to Chinese Metaphysics mastery!

Introduction - Earth Day Masters

Silence is golden, and Earth Day Masters best illustrate this example.

Earth Day Masters are quiet and tough, and can therefore be trusted to keep secrets or act as confidantes. This of course means that they are also sincere in their intentions, and equally wise in their thoughts. They just do not yield or share their thoughts easily, though.

Wu 戊 Earth Day Masters make dependable and steady friends, although they can also be quite stubborn and unwavering in their stance. Since Wu Earth is also Yang Earth, Wu Earth types are also tough and rugged by nature, although they can also possess an amazing degree of tolerance of circumstances and others.

Ji 己 Earth Day Masters are productive, tolerant and resourceful, and tend to be more understanding of the weaknesses and fallacies of others. They however lack the ability to make quick, spontaneous decisions when needed – due to their lack of adaptability. They are, however, relatively gentler, more yielding and receptive in nature, compared to their Wu Earth counterparts – due to Ji Earth's Yin nature.

Wu (戊) Earth Day Master

Overview:

Wu 戊 Earth is Yang Earth. Examples of Wu Earth include large, looming mountains as well as huge chunks of rock and earth. Being thick and solid by nature, Wu Earth has the capacity to counter and even control Water. A good example of such is when a dam is used to contain water in a reservoir.

Where both Fire and Wood are present in a Wu Earth Day Master's BaZi Chart, it would suffice to say that this Day Master's Wealth and Officer Stars shall be strong and thriving. And under such circumstances, this Day Master has great potential to achieve significant success in life.

There are different interpretations and theories, however, regarding Earth that contains Metal, Wood, Water and Fire hidden within, especially if this Day Master happens to be born in a Chen (Dragon), Xu (Dog), Chou (Ox) or Wei (Goat) Month – i.e. the Four Storages or Graveyard Earthly Branches.

Wu Earth Day Masters make dependable and steady friends, although they can also be quite stubborn and unwavering in their stance. Being Yang Earth, Wu Earth types are also tough and rugged by nature; although they can also possess an amazing degree of tolerance of circumstances and others.

Wu 戊 Earth Day Master, Born in First Month 正月

Yin 寅 (Tiger) Month
February 4th – March 5th

Do note that the dates provided above are subject to slight yearly variations. Please refer to the Ten Thousand Year Calendar for the accurate transition dates for each year.

Day Master Wu 戊 Earth　　　**Month** Yin 寅 (Tiger)

正月 First Month

Tiger

日元 Day Master	月 Month
戊 *Wu* **Yang Earth**	寅 *Yin* **Tiger** **Yang Wood**

For a Wu Earth Day Master born in a Yin (Tiger) Month, a Seven Killings Structure is formed where Jia Wood is revealed as one of the Heavenly Stems.

Where Bing Fire is revealed as one of the Heavenly Stems, an Indirect Resource Structure is formed.

Where Wu Earth is revealed as one of the Heavenly Stems, a Thriving Structure is formed when the conditions are completely met and supported.

Should, however, neither Jia Wood, Bing Fire nor Wu Earth happen to be revealed within the Heavenly Stems, one should select the BaZi Chart's most prominent Qi attribute at one's discretion.

| Day Master | Wu 戊 Earth | Month | Yin 寅 (Tiger) |

喜用神提要 Regulating Useful God Reference Guide

月 Month	用神 Useful God
1st Month 正月 Yin 寅 (Tiger) Month	丙 *Bing* **Yang Fire** 　甲 *Jia* **Yang Wood** 　癸 *Gui* **Yin Water**

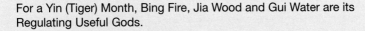

For a Yin (Tiger) Month, Bing Fire, Jia Wood and Gui Water are its Regulating Useful Gods.

It would be impossible for Wu Earth to be produced and strengthened, should the 'light' and 'warmth' provided by Bing Fire happen to be missing.

Similarly, without Jia Wood to 'loosen' and 'plough' it, the usefulness (or quality) of Wu Earth would also be extremely limited.

Without Gui Water to 'moisten' it, Wu Earth would also be unable to play its role in sustaining and nourishing 'life'.

As such, Bing Fire is the primary Useful God to this Wu Earth Day Master, with Jia Wood and Gui Water as the secondary Useful Gods.

正月 First Month

Tiger

| Day Master | Wu 戊 Earth | Month | Yin 寅 (Tiger) |

4th day of February – 5th day of March, Gregorian Calendar

Where Jia Wood, Bing Fire and Gui Waterare all present as in the chart, it would hence be possible for Earth to be 'loosened', produced and duly supported. This would be a superior chart.

A Wu Earth Day Master born in an hour where Fire and Earth Qi are present will do well with some Water Qi in his or her BaZi Chart.

Where Metal and Water Qi are present in abundance, this chart would do well with some Fire Qi.

A Day Master born in a Wu (Horse) Hour would denote that the formation of a Fire Structure be very likely. And since Metal is the Useful God in producing Water, it would certainly serve as an important Useful God to this Day Master.

| Day Master | Wu 戊 Earth | Month | Yin 寅 (Tiger) |

Commentary

In addition to the preceding narratives on the potential Structures and scenarios resulting from a Wu Earth Day Master born in a Yin (Tiger) Month, the following circumstances also play their respective roles in determining the overall strength of this Day Master's BaZi Chart.

Tiger

Note:

- Where the Wu earth penetrates to the Heavenly Stem and the Earthly Branches are occupied mainly by Earth Qi there is hinder danger in the chart.

- In this month, Wood Qi is also very strong, it might 'clash' with the abundant Earth Qi, with neither emerging stronger than the other in this tussle. There is, however, the possibility and risk of having a 'landslide' of sorts caused by Earth in the chart. Not a good feature to be found. This is why Bing Fire is needed to provide 'warmth' to this Wu Earth Day Master and divert the Wood to Earth Qi smoothly. Then and only then will this Day Master be a strong, thriving one.

- The preceding scenario much depends on the quality of Jia Wood to support the Bing Fire which in turn, produces Wu Earth.

- Where only Wood Structures are seen in this Chart, Geng Metal would still be needed as a Useful God in order to keep Wood under control. Where Metal is employed as a Useful God in the absence of Water, this Day Master may tend to be accident-prone.

- Where Bing Fire and Gui Water are seen in the Heavenly Stems – but both are not found side-by-side – a 'standard' or 'conventional' match between both elements takes place.

- Where the Yin (Tiger), Wu (Horse) and Xu (Dog) Earthly Branches form a Fire Structure, Gui Water should preferably also be seen penetrating through the Heavenly Stems. Under such circumstances, Gui Water serves as the primary Useful God to this Wu Earth Day Master, with Bing Fire as its secondary Useful God.

- Where the Earthly Branches form a Fire Structure – with Jia Wood revealed in the Heavenly Stems but Gui Water not – this Wu Earth Day Master may have to toil and slog through the earlier stages of his or her life, before he or she ultimately succeeds and becomes wealthy.

- Where Water is missing from the chart, this Wu Earth Day Master may be afflicted by loneliness in life.

- Where this Day Master encounters additional Wood – which forms a dominant Wood formation – and while Fire is also revealed in the Heavenly Stems at the same time – this is a noble and superior chart. Without Bing Fire penetrating through the Heavenly Stems, this Wu Earth Day Master may only lead an average life at best.

- Where Geng Metal is revealed in the Heavenly Stems, this Wu Earth Day Master shall prosper in life.

- Where the Earthly Branches form a Wood Structure – with Wood also revealed in the Heavenly Stems, but Earth (a Companion Star) and Fire (a Resource Star) are missing from the chart– a Follow the Killings Structure may be formed.

| Day Master | Wu 戊 Earth | Month | Yin 寅 (Tiger) |

Additional Attributes

格局 Structural Star	偏印 Indirect Resource	七殺 Seven Killings
用神 Useful God	Bing 丙 Fire	Jia 甲 Wood
Conditions	Where both this Day Master's Seven Killings and Indirect Resource Stars are simultaneously seen, the quality of this chart is superior.	
Positive Circumstances	Gui Water should preferably be present as well. In its absence, this Day Master may start-off prosperous in life, although his or her fortunes later on may be unstable.	
Negative Circumstances	Absence of Bing Fire in the chart.	

格局 Structural Star	偏印 Indirect Resource	正財 Direct Wealth
用神 Useful God	Bing 丙 Fire	Gui 癸 Water
Conditions	Where only the Indirect Resource Structure is formed, Gui Water (Direct Wealth Star) can be used as a Useful God. (Where Ren Water is also revealed in the Heavenly Stems, this Day Master shall enjoy long lasting prosperity.)	
Positive Circumstances	Presence of Ren Water in the chart.	
Negative Circumstances	Bing Fire and Gui Water are side-by-side in the Heavenly Stems.	

Day Master	Wu 戊 Earth		Month	Yin 寅 (Tiger)

Additional Attributes

格局 Structural Star	七殺 Seven Killings	食神 Eating God
用神 Useful God	Jia 甲 Wood	Geng 庚 Metal
Conditions	Where only the Seven Killings Structure is formed, with the absence of Bing Fire as a favourable Indirect Resource Star, Geng Metal – an Eating God Star – should be selected as the Useful God.	
Positive Circumstances	Presence of Bing Fire in the chart.	
Negative Circumstances	The absence of Geng Metal.	

格局 Structural Star	正官 Direct Officer
用神 Useful God	Yi 乙 Wood
Conditions	Yi Wood (Direct Officer Star) combines with Geng Metal (Eating God Star) to form Metal. Under such circumstances, this Day Master may lack sincerity.
Positive Circumstances	-
Negative Circumstances	-

*   *Bing Fire is the most-preferred Useful God for a Wu Earth Day Master born in a Yin (Tiger) Month.*

***Jia Wood and Gui Water are the secondary Useful Gods.*

正月 First Month

Tiger

| Day Master | Wu 戊 Earth | | Month | Yin 寅 (Tiger) |

Summary

- The absence of Geng Metal (Eating God Star) – for a Wu Earth-Wu (Horse) Day Master born in a Yin (Tiger) Month would be unfavorable. The person lacks ideas and purpose in life.

- Where the Earthly Branches form a Wood Structure, it may be possible for a Follow the Killings Structure to be formed when there are absolutely no support for the Earth element.

- Where the Earthly Branches form a Fire (Resource) Structure – but Ren Water and Gui Water are missing – this Day Master may be afflicted by loneliness in life.

Wu 戊 Earth Day Master, Born in Second Month 二月

Mao 卯 (Rabbit) Month
March 6th – April 4th

Do note that the dates provided above are subject to slight yearly variations. Please refer to the Ten Thousand Year Calendar for the accurate transition dates for each year.

二
月

Second Month

卯
Rabbit

| Day Master | Wu 戊 Earth | | Month | Mao 卯 (Rabbit) |

日元 Day Master	月 Month
戊 *Wu* **Yang Earth**	卯 *Mao* **Rabbit** **Yin Wood**

For a Wu Earth Day Master born in a Mao (Rabbit) Month, a Direct Officer Structure is formed where Yi Wood is revealed as one of the Heavenly Stems.

Even if Yi Wood does not penetrate through the Heavenly Stem, Direct Officer Structure is still considered to have been formed.

| Day Master | Wu 戊 Earth | | Month | Mao 卯 (Rabbit) |

喜用神提要 **Regulating Useful God Reference Guide**

月 Month	用神 Useful God
2nd Month 二月 Mao 卯 (Rabbit) Month	丙 *Bing* **Yang Fire** 甲 *Jia* **Yang Wood** 癸 *Gui* **Yin Water**

Rabbit

For a Mao (Rabbit) Month, Bing Fire, Jia Wood and Gui Water are its Regulating Useful Gods.

It would be impossible for Wu Earth to be healthy, should the 'light' and 'warmth' provided by Bing Fire be missing.

Similarly, without Jia Wood to 'loosen' and 'plough' it, the usefulness of Wu Earth would also be extremely limited.

Without Gui Water to 'moisten' it, Wu Earth would also be unable to play its role in sustaining and nourishing 'life'.

As such, Bing Fire is the primary Useful God to this Wu Earth Day Master, with Jia Wood and Gui Water as the secondary Useful Gods.

BaZi Structures & Structural Useful Gods 格局與格局用神

Day Master Wu 戊 Earth	Month Mao 卯 (Rabbit)

6th day of March – 4th day of April, Gregorian Calendar

A Wu Earth Day Master born in a Mao (Rabbit) Month forms the Direct Officer Structure in his or her BaZi Chart. This is because Wood – amongst the Five Elements – is at its peak or most prosperous, this Month.

Fire is hence needed to keep Wood under control, and also produce and support this Day Master. It would also be best for a Direct Officer and Direct Resource Star to be seen together, as both will produce and support this Day Master.

Rabbit

Wood (an Officer Star) – in a Mao (Rabbit) Month – is very strong. This would surely result in Earth falling under the control of Wood. It would, however, be better to use Fire instead of Metal as this Day Master's Useful God. This is because although Metal has the ability to 'slice' and weaken Wood, it also has the tendency to weaken Earth.

| Day Master | Wu 戊 Earth | | Month | Mao 卯 (Rabbit) |

Commentary

In addition to the preceding narratives on the potential Structures and scenarios resulting from a Wu Earth Day Master born in a Mao (Rabbit) Month, the following circumstances also play their respective roles in determining the overall strength of this Day Master's BaZi Chart.

Note:

• Yi Wood – a Direct Officer Star – is strong in a Mao (Rabbit) Month.

• Where only one Yi Wood is present in the stem, however, it would be impossible for a Follow the Killings Structure to be formed.

Rabbit

• Where Geng Metal is also revealed in the Heavenly Stems, it would combine with Yi Wood to form Metal. This is undersirable because the Metal Qi is weak during this month. Hence such formation is only surface level, resulting in the person being dishonest and insincere.

• Where an abundance of Yi Woods (Direct Officer Star) – are seen in the chart, a condition known as Guan Duo Bian Gui 官多變鬼 (Many Officers Morphing to Ghosts) – or Quan Guan Hui Dang 權官會党 (Powerful Officers Encountering a Crowd) takes place. Should Geng Metal, however, happen to be present as well, this Wu Earth Day Master may lack sincerity in his or her intentions; regardless of how he or she may appear outwardly to others. This Day Master may also be prone towards making empty promises, while also possessing a greedy disposition that would make it hard for him or her to make friends.

• A best-case scenario for this Wu Earth Day Master would be where the Earthly Branches encounter Jia Wood, which forms a soft Seven Killings Structure with this Day Master . Should Geng Metal happen to be missing, however, this Day Master would only lead a normal, average life at best. Geng Metal and Jia Wood must go hand-in-hand with Wu Earth for this month.

二月 Second Month

Rabbit

Day Master	Wu 戊 Earth		Month	Mao 卯 (Rabbit)
Additional Attributes				

格局 **Structural Star**	正財 Direct Wealth
用神 **Useful God**	Gui 癸 Water
Conditions	Where Gui Water is used together with Bing Fire – this person may wield power and wealth.
Positive Circumstances	Presence of Bing Fire
Negative Circumstances	Bing Fire is next to Gui Water.

Day Master	Wu 戊 Earth	Month	Mao 卯 (Rabbit)

Additional Attributes

格局 **Structural Star**	正官 Direct Officer
用神 **Useful God**	Yi 乙 Wood
Conditions	Where Jia Wood (Seven Killings Star) – meets Yi Wood (Direct Officer Star) – this Day Master may lack motivation and the drive to succeed in life.
Positive Circumstances	Geng Metal combines with Yi Wood to form Metal.
Negative Circumstances	Presence of Jia and Yi Wood side by side in the chart.

* *Bing Fire and Gui Water are the preferred Useful Gods for a Wu Earth Day Master born in a Mao (Rabbit) Month.*

二月 Second Month

Rabbit

二月 Second Month

卯 Rabbit

| Day Master | Wu 戊 Earth | Month | Mao 卯 (Rabbit) |

Summary

- It would be unfavorable, should Geng Metal missing in the chart.

- Where this Day Master's Direct Officer and Seven Killings Stars are simultaneously present, it is preferred the Direct Officer Stars remain, and the Seven Killings Stars be combined away.

- Where both Direct Officer and Seven Killings Stars are present, the present of one Geng Metal element would suffice to combine Yi Wood (Direct Officer) away.

- Jia Wood – a Seven Killings Star – plays a prominent role in influencing the strength and quality of this Wu Earth Day Master.

- Where Jia Wood and Yi Wood are both seen, their collusive influence on this Day Master there would be confusion to the personality of this person.

- It would be ideal and favorable to this Day Master, should both its Seven Killings and Direct Resource Stars happen to be simultaneously present.

Wu 戊 Earth Day Master, Born in Third Month 三月

Chen 辰 (Dragon) Month
April 5th - May 5th

Do note that the dates provided above are subject to slight yearly variations. Please refer to the Ten Thousand Year Calendar for the accurate transition dates for each year.

三月 Third Month

Dragon

| Day Master | Wu 戊 Earth | Month | Chen 辰 (Dragon) |

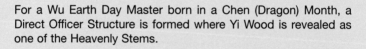

日元 Day Master	月 Month

戊
Wu
Yang Earth

辰
Chen
Dragon
Yang Earth

For a Wu Earth Day Master born in a Chen (Dragon) Month, a Direct Officer Structure is formed where Yi Wood is revealed as one of the Heavenly Stems.

Where Gui Water is revealed as one of the Heavenly Stems, a Direct Wealth Structure is formed.

Where Wu Earth is revealed as one of the Heavenly Stems, a Thriving Structure may be formed when the conditions are right.

Should, however, neither Yi Wood, Wu Earth nor Gui Water happen to be revealed within the Heavenly Stems, one should select a Structure according to the BaZi Chart's most prominent Qi attribute at one's discretion.

Day Master Wu 戊 Earth   **Month** Chen 辰 (Dragon)

喜用神提要 Regulating Useful God Reference Guide

三月 Third Month

Dragon

月 Month	用神 Useful God		
3rd Month 三月 **Chen** 辰 **(Dragon) Month**	甲 *Jia* **Yang Wood**	丙 *Bing* **Yang Fire**	癸 *Gui* **Yin Water**

For a Chen (Dragon) Month, Jia Wood, Bing Fire and Gui Water are its most important Regulating Useful Gods.

In the case of this Day Master, Jia Wood should first be used to 'loosen' and 'plough' the Earth.

Bing Fire and Gui Water, meanwhile, serve as the conditioning secondary Useful Gods to this Day Master.

BaZi Structures & Structural Useful Gods 格局與格局用神

Day Master	Wu 戊 Earth	Month	Chen 辰 (Dragon)

5th day of April – 5th day of May, Gregorian Calendar

Dragon

The Chen (Dragon) Earthly Branch – in the case of a Wu Metal Day Master born in a Chen (Dragon) Month – contains the Hidden Stems of Wu Earth, Yi Wood and Gui Water. Earth and Wood Qi are prominent in a Chen (Dragon) Month.

Water is also a necessary Useful God for this Wu Earth Day Master. This is to keep the Earth moist and fertile. Fertile Earth denotes prosperity and abundance.

Where Water is present, Wood may then be used in tandem with it as the Useful God. If this condition is met, this Day Master shall enjoy fame, status and authority in life.

Where Metal is selected as the Useful God based on the conditions of the chart, this Day Master shall also enjoy prosperity in life. This is because Metal and Water are a sentimental combination working in tandem to nourish, plough and nurture the Earth. A spectacular life is expected.

Day Master	Wu 戊 Earth	Month	Chen 辰 (Dragon)

Commentary

In addition to the preceding narratives on the potential Structures and scenarios resulting from a Wu Earth Day Master born in a Chen (Dragon) Month, the following circumstances also play their respective roles in determining the overall strength of this Day Master's BaZi Chart.

Note:

- The Chen (Dragon) Month also serves as storage for excess Water Qi.

- Where Jia Wood and Gui Water are revealed in the Heavenly Stems this Day Master shall enjoy fame and fortune in life. This is of course subject to the condition that Bing Fire is also revealed as a supporting or auxiliary Useful God.

- Where Jia Wood and Bing Fire are both missing from the chart – and while there is also no Gui Water penetrating through the Heavenly Stems – this Day Master may lead a life devoid of a sense of purpose and direction.

- Where Bing Fire is revealed in the Heavenly Stems but Gui Water is not, this Day Master may prosper and become wealthy early in life; although his or her wealth may not be sustainable and he or she may even be afflicted by poverty later in life.

- Where Fire is present in abundance in the Earthly Branches – but Gui Water (Wealth Star) is revealed instead of Bing Fire in the Heavenly Stems – this Day Master shall succeed and become wealthy later in life; although he or she may have to toil and struggle in the earlier stages of life.

- Where the Earthly Branches form a Wood Structure, with Geng Metal also revealed in the Heavenly Stems, this Day Master shall succeed in his or her life's pursuits.

- Where Fire and Metal are completely missing from the chart, Wood and Earth may clash and conflict with one another in this Day Master's BaZi Chart. Under such circumstances, this Day Master may be susceptible to stomach-related ailments.

- Where wood is in abundance, the Self Element is weak. This Day Master will correspondingly be susceptible to leading a life of poverty and poor health.

三
月

Third Month

Dragon

23

三月 **Third Month**

Dragon

| Day Master | Wu 戊 Earth | | Month | Chen 辰 (Dragon) |

Additional Attributes

格局 Structural Star	七殺 Seven Killings	正財 Direct Wealth	偏印 Indirect Resource
用神 Useful God	Jia 甲 Wood	Gui 癸 Water	Bing 丙 Fire
Conditions	The best possible structures in this Day Master's BaZi Chart would be formed, where Gui Water (Direct Wealth Star) produces Jia Wood (Seven Killings Star). The second-best structure would be where Jia Wood (Seven Killings Star) produces Bing Fire (Indirect Resource Star). Where Bing Fire is revealed while Jia Wood remains hidden and Gui Water absent – this Day Master shall still prosper and become wealthy in life. But there would be equal share of difficulties and hurdles along the way.		
Positive Circumstances	Where there is no Gui Water (Direct Wealth Star), Ren Water (Indirect Wealth Star) may be used as a substitute. Under such circumstances, however, this Day Master may have to scrimp through early life, especially where basic necessities such as food and clothes are concerned.		
Negative Circumstances	Without Ren Water or Gui Water, this Day Master may find it difficult to prosper in life.		

Day Master	Wu 戊 Earth	Month	Chen 辰 (Dragon)

Additional Attributes

格局 **Structural Star**	七殺 Seven Killings	正官 Direct Officer
用神 **Useful God**	Jia 甲 Wood	Yi 乙 Wood
Conditions	Where the Earthly Branches form a Wood Structure, it would be likely for a Seven Killing Structure to be inadvertenly formed, instead of a Direct Officer Structure. It would then be favourable for this Day Master, to have Geng Metal at the Heavenly Stems.	
Positive Circumstances	Where a Follow the Killings Structure is formed, all Five Elements must also be present in the chart. If one were to be missing or absent, it would be difficult for this Day Master to succeed in life.	
Negative Circumstances	There is no Geng Metal present in the BaZi Chart.	

* Jia Wood, Gui Water and Bing Fire are the preferred Useful Gods for a Wu Earth Day Master born in a Chen (Dragon) Month.

Dragon

三月 Third Month

25

三月 **Third Month**

| Day Master | Wu 戊 Earth | Month | Chen 辰 (Dragon) |

Summary

- Where Jia Wood, Gui Water and Bing Fire are missing from the Four Pillars of Destiny, this Day Master may be susceptible to poor health and chronic illness in life. He or she may also lack a sense of purpose or direction in life.

Dragon

Wu 戊 Earth Day Master, Born in Fourth Month 四月

Si 巳 (Snake) Month
May 6th - June 5th

Do note that the dates provided above are subject to slight yearly variations. Please refer to the Ten Thousand Year Calendar for the accurate transition dates for each year.

Snake

| Day Master | Wu 戊 Earth | Month | Si 巳 (Snake) |

日元 Day Master	月 Month
戊 *Wu* **Yang Earth**	巳 *Si* **Snake** **Yin Fire**

For a Wu Earth Day Master born in a Si (Snake) Month, the Earthly Branch of Si (Snake) is Wu Earth's 'Prosperous' position. The absolute Thriving Structure is formed.

Where Bing Fire or the Wu Earth is revealed as one of the Heavenly Stems, a Thriving Structure is formed.

Where Geng Metal is revealed as one of the Heavenly Stems, an Eating Structure may be formed when the conditions are completely met and supported by the Earthly branches.

| Day Master | Wu 戊 Earth | Month | Si 巳 (Snake) |

喜用神提要 **Regulating Useful God Reference Guide**

月 Month	用神 Useful God
4th Month 四月 Si 巳 (Snake) Month	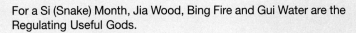甲 *Jia* **Yang Wood** 丙 *Bing* **Yang Fire** 癸 *Gui* **Yin Water**

Snake

For a Si (Snake) Month, Jia Wood, Bing Fire and Gui Water are the Regulating Useful Gods.

Since the Si (Snake) Earthly Branch is also Wu Earth's 'Prosperous' position, Jia Wood should first be employed to 'loosen' and 'plough' Earth.

Bing Fire and Gui Water, meanwhile, serve as secondary Useful Gods to this Day Master.

BaZi Structures & Structural Useful Gods 格局與格局用神

| Day Master | Wu 戊 Earth | Month | Si 巳 (Snake) |

6th day of May – 5th day of June, Gregorian Calendar

四月 Fourth Month

Snake

Wu Earth Day Master born in a Si (Snake) summer month, the Si (Snake) Earthly Branch is Wu Earth's 'Prosperous' position.

Fire is obviously strong and 'blazing' in a summer month. Since both Fire and Earth are strong in a Si (Snake) Month, Metal and Water will consequently tend to be 'parched' or even 'dry' to the point of extinction.

As such, Water would first be needed to 'moisten' this Day Master.

Here, the Geng Metal Hidden Stem found inside the Si (Snake) Earthly Branch may also be selected as a Useful God, in order to produce and ensure the continuity of Water. If Metal is strong, this chart is beautiful.

Where Water is present but Metal absent, this Wu Earth Day Master would be lacking, in terms of balance and strength. Under such circumstances, this Day Master may still prosper and become wealthy in life; although his or her wealth may not be sustainable or lasting.

This Wu Earth Day Master should avoid encountering additional Fire Qi since Fire does further weakens Metal, which is needed to produce Water as this Day Master's Useful God. It would equally be unfavorable for this Day Master to have Wood present in abundance – since Wood produces Fire.

Water in abundance is however welcome.

Day Master	Wu 戊 Earth		Month	Si 巳 (Snake)

Commentary

In addition to the preceding narratives on the potential Structures and scenarios resulting from a Wu Earth Day Master born in a Si (Snake) Month, the following circumstances also play their respective roles in determining the overall strength of this Day Master's BaZi Chart.

Note:

- Gui Water is the primary Useful God for this Wu Earth Day Master, with Bing Fire and Jia Wood serving as secondary Useful Gods.

- Where possible, this Day Master should avoid encountering additional Fire and 'dry' or 'parched' Earth Qi.

- Where only Fire and Earth happen to be present in the Heavenly Stems, Fire would hence be 'hot' and 'blazing' while Earth would be 'dry' or 'parched'. Under such circumstances, this Day Master may be afflicted by loneliness and hardship in life.

- Where only Gui Water is available as a Useful God and, this Day Master shall possess a strong sense of independence and determination to succeed. Despite the circumstances, he or she will still make good in life.

- Where Jia Wood is revealed in the Heavenly Stems, this person would enjoy prosperity and wealth throughout life.

- Without Gui Water, this person would only lead an average life at best.

- Where the Si (Snake), Chou (Ox) and You (Rooster) Earthly Branches form a Metal Structure – while Gui Water is also revealed in the Heavenly Stems this Day Master shall be a skillful, knowledgeable one and excel in whatever pursuit he or she may choose in life.

四月

Fourth Month

Snake

31

🐍
Snake

Day Master	Wu 戊 Earth		Month	Si 巳 (Snake)

Additional Attributes

格局 Structural Star	偏印 Indirect Resource	七殺 Seven Killings	正財 Direct Wealth
用神 Useful God	Bing 丙 Fire	Jia 甲 Wood	Gui 癸 Water
Conditions	Gui Water (Direct Wealth Star) produces Jia Wood (Seven Killings Star). Jia Wood (Seven Killings Star) produces Bing Fire (Indirect Resource Star). Where all three Useful Gods are present, this Day Master shall immense success and good fortune.		
Positive Circumstances	Presence of Gui Water.		
Negative Circumstances	Where only Bing Fire (Indirect Resource Star) is present – while both Ren Water and Gui Water are missing. This Day Master may be afflicted by loneliness and poverty in life.		

| Day Master | Wu 戊 Earth | Month | Si 巳 (Snake) |

Additional Attributes

四月 Fourth Month

Snake

格局 Structural Star	食神 Eating God	傷官 Hurting Officer
用神 Useful God	Geng 庚 Metal	Xin 辛 Metal
Conditions	Where the relevant Earthly Branches form Metal – which in turn, forms Eating God and Hurting Officer Structures with this Day Master – Gui Water is needed to penetrate through the Heavenly Stems.	
Positive Circumstances	Gui Water is preferred to Ren Water, as a Useful God to this Day Master.	
Negative Circumstances	-	

* *Gui Water is the primary Useful God for a Wu Earth Day Master born in a Si (Snake) Month.*

** *Bing Fire and Jia Wood serve as secondary Useful Gods to this Day Master.*

33

四月 Fourth Month

Snake

Day Master	Wu 戊 Earth	Month	Si 巳 (Snake)

Summary

- Where Gui Water is employed as a Useful God, it would be best if Shen (Monkey) and Hai (Pig) are also present as Earthly Branches in this Wu Earth Day Master's BaZi Chart.

Wu 戊 Earth Day Master, Born in Fifth Month 五月

Wu 午 (Horse) Month
June 6th - July 6th

Do note that the dates provided above are subject to slight yearly variations. Please refer to the Ten Thousand Year Calendar for the accurate transition dates for each year.

五月 Fifth Month

Horse

| Day Master | Wu 戊 Earth | Month | Wu 午 (Horse) |

日元 Day Master	月 Month
戊 *Wu* **Yang Earth**	午 *Wu* **Horse** **Yang Fire**

For a Wu Earth Day Master born in a Wu (Horse) Month, a Direct Resource Structure is formed where Ding Fire is revealed as one of the Heavenly Stems.

Where the Ji Earth is revealed in the Heavenly Stems and the overall setup permitting and supporting, the Goat Blade Structure is formed.

Should, however, Ding Fire and Ji Earth are both not revealed within the Heavenly Stems, the Direct Resource Structure is assumed.

Day Master	Wu 戊 Earth	Month	Wu 午 (Horse)

喜用神提要 Regulating Useful God Reference Guide

月 Month	用神 Useful God
5th Month 五月 Wu 午 (Horse) Month	壬 *Ren* **Yang Water** 甲 *Jia* **Yang Wood** 丙 *Bing* **Yang Fire**

Horse

For a Wu (Horse) Month, Ren Water, Jia Wood and Bing Fire are the Regulating Useful Gods.

It is important to 'regulate' the overall Qi of this Wu Earth Day Master's BaZi Chart. To achieve this objective, Ren Water should be employed as the primary Useful God, with Jia Wood and Bing Fire simultaneously employed as secondary Useful Gods.

五
月

Fifth Month

Horse

BaZi Structures & Structural Useful Gods 格局與格局用神

| Day Master | Wu 戊 Earth | Month | Wu 午 (Horse) |

6th day of June – 6th day of July, Gregorian Calendar

Wu Earth Day Master born in a Wu (Horse) Month, Earth may be depicted as a horizontal, flat strip of 'parched', 'dry' land. Fire and Earth Qi are extremely strong in this Month.

As such, where Earth meets Water Qi, the latter will serve to 'moisten' and 'irrigate' the former. Where Earth meets Metal, however, Metal would invariably be 'melted' and weakened by the strong Fire Qi present.

Both Metal and Water would therefore have to be rooted in their respective elements, so that their continuity and relevance as Useful Gods to this Day Master may be ensured.

A Day Master born in an hour where Metal and Water happen to be strong may hence be 'moistened' accordingly.

This Day Master should avoid encountering additional Fire, Wood and Earth Qi as much as possible.

Wood, however, represents the Spouse or Husband Star for female Wu Earth Day Masters. Water would hence be needed to produce and 'protect' Wood. There is also a need to watch out for an abundance of Fire, since it would counter Water.

| Day Master | Wu 戊 Earth | Month | Wu 午 (Horse) |

Commentary

In addition to the preceding narratives on the potential Structures and scenarios resulting from a Wu Earth Day Master born in a Wu (Horse) Month, the following circumstances also play their respective roles in determining the overall strength of this Day Master's BaZi Chart.

Note:

- Ren Water is the primary Useful God for this Wu Earth Day Master. Jia Wood serves as the secondary Useful God to this Day Master.

- It is undesirable to see Ji Earth penetrating through the Heavenly Stems.

- Wood in a summer month simply cannot do without Ren Water, just as Earth in a summer month cannot do without Jia Wood. The best-case scenario would of course be where Ren Water and Jia Wood are both revealed in the Heavenly Stems.

- In a Wu (Horse) Month, Xin Metal would be the ideal choice of Useful God, to produce Ren Water.

- Where Wood and Fire are in abundance in the chart – while Water is conspicuously absent – this Day Master may lead a simple and average life at best, although possibly a very lonely and sad one as well.

- It is undesirable for Ji Earth – a Rob Wealth Star – to be seen penetrating through the Heavenly Stems. This forms the Goat Blade structure and at the same time, the Ji Earth would also 'split' and weaken the capacity of Ren Water and Jia Wood to serve as Useful Gods to this Day Master.

五
月

Fifth Month

Horse

39

五月 Fifth Month

Horse

Day Master Wu 戊 Earth		Month Wu 午 (Horse)

Additional Attributes

格局 Structural Star	偏財 Indirect Wealth	七殺 Seven Killings
用神 Useful God	Ren 壬 Water	Jia 甲 Wood
Conditions	Xin Metal is the preferred choice to have, as the Heavenly Stem of the Year Pillar. Metal keeps the Water flowing.	
Positive Circumstances	Presence of rooted Xin Metal.	
Negative Circumstances	In the absence of Ren Water, Jia Wood – which forms a Seven Killings Structure with this Day Master – would be ineffective as a Useful God.	

Day Master	Wu 戊 Earth	Month	Wu 午 (Horse)

Additional Attributes

Horse

格局 Structural Star	偏印 Indirect Resource	正印 Direct Resource
用神 Useful God	Bing 丙 Fire	Ding 丁 Fire
Conditions	Where the Earthly Branches forms Fire formation – while having Ren Water penetrating through the Heavenly Stems, this Day Master shall be a knowledgeable and skilful one.	
Positive Circumstances	Ren Water is preferred to Gui Water, as a Useful God.	
Negative Circumstances	Should neither Ren Water nor Gui Water penetrate through the Heavenly Stems, this Day Master would still be skilful and learned, although his or her skills would not serve him or her well in life.	

* Ren Water is the primary Useful God for a Wu Earth Day Master born in a Wu (Horse) Month.

** Jia Wood and Bing Fire serve as secondary Useful Gods to this Day Master.

*** It would also be preferable to avoid having additional Earth countering and exerting an overly strong control over Ren Water.

五月 Fifth Month

Day Master	Wu 戊 Earth	Month	Wu 午 (Horse)

Summary

- Ren Water (Indirect Wealth Star) - is the primary Useful God for this Wu Earth Day Master.

- Regardless of any structure that may be formed in the BaZi Chart, Water must be seen penetrating through the Heavenly Stems.

- It is undesirable for Ji Earth – the Rob Wealth Star – to be revealed in the Heavenly Stems. This is because it has the potential to 'destroy' or wreak havoc to the Water stars in the chart.

- Where Water is missing or lacking, this Day Master may lead a life of suffering and difficulty.

- Ren Water is preferred to Gui Water as a Useful God to this Day Master.

- Where present, the Zi (Rat) and Wu (Horse) Earthly Branches should not be side by side.

- No Wu Earth Day Master may thrive or survive, without the assistance of Metal and Water in her BaZi Chart.

Horse

Wu 戊 Earth Day Master, Born in Sixth Month 六月

Wei 未 (Goat) Month
July 7th - August 7th

Do note that the dates provided above are subject to slight yearly variations. Please refer to the Ten Thousand Year Calendar for the accurate transition dates for each year.

| Day Master Wu 戊 Earth | Month Wei 未 (Goat) |

Goat

日元 Day Master	月 Month
戊 *Wu* **Yang Earth**	未 *Wei* **Goat** **Yin Earth**

For a Wu Earth Day Master born in a Wei (Goat) Month, a Direct Resource Structure is formed where Ding Fire is revealed as one of the Heavenly Stems.

Where Yi Wood is revealed as one of the Heavenly Stems, a Direct Officer Structure is formed.

Where Ji Earth is revealed as one of the Heaenly Stems, a Goat Glade Structure may be formed depending on the circumstances.

Should, however, neither Yi Wood, Ji Earth nor Ding Fire happen to be revealed within the Heavenly Stems, one should select the BaZi Chart's most prominent Qi attribute at one's discretion.

| Day Master | Wu 戊 Earth | | Month | Wei 未 (Goat) |

喜用神提要 Regulating Useful God Reference Guide

月 Month	用神 Useful God
6th Month 六月 Wei 未 (Goat) Month	癸 *Gui* **Yin Water** 丙 *Bing* **Yang Fire** 甲 *Jia* **Yang Wood**

Goat

For a Wei (Goat) Month, Gui Water, Bing Fire and Jia Wood are the Regulating Useful Gods.

It is important to 'regulate' the overall Qi of this Wu Earth Day Master's BaZi Chart.

As such, Gui Water must be present, if this objective is to be achieved. It must also be used together with Bing Fire, to bring about the desired effect.

Since Earth is also 'leaden' or 'heavy' in a Wei (Goat) Month, Jia Wood must not be missing as well.

BaZi Structures & Structural Useful Gods 格局與格局用神

Day Master	Wu 戊 Earth	Month	Wei 未 (Goat)

7th day of July – 7th day of August, Gregorian Calendar

In a Wei (Goat) Month falls in late summer, Earth is very hot and dry.

Since Earth is 'thick' and 'dry' in a Wei (Goat) Month, it would invariably compete amongst itself for Water.

As such, Water is the primary and most important Useful God for this Day Master. Where Water is available to 'moisten' Earth, the latter would hence be able to produce Metal.

Yi Wood represents the Spouse or Husband Star for female Wu Earth Day Masters. Water – when revealed and penetrating through the Heavenly Stems – will bring about good wealth and relationship luck prospects for female Day Masters, especially with their husbands.

Goat

| Day Master | Wu 戊 Earth | | Month | Wei 未 (Goat) |

Commentary

In addition to the preceding narratives on the potential Structures and scenarios resulting from a Wu Earth Day Master born in a Wei (Goat) Month, the following circumstances also play their respective roles in determining the overall strength of this Day Master's BaZi Chart.

Note:

- Gui Water is the primary Useful God for this Wu Earth Day Master, with Bing Fire and Jia Wood as the secondary Useful Gods. This Day Master shares the similar Useful Gods as its counterpart born in a Si (Snake) Month.

- Earth is the strongest element in a Wei (Goat) Month. As such, Jia Wood – as a Useful God – is needed to 'loosen' Earth. Nevertheless, Jia Wood in a summer month will still need Ren Water and Gui Water, as supporting Useful Gods. Otherwise the wood would not survive.

- Where Metal Qi is abundant in this chart, more attention should be diverted towards employing Bing Fire to keep Metal under control.

- Where Jia Wood, Bing Fire and Gui Water are all revealed in the Heavenly Stems, this Day Master shall not only prosper and become wealthy; he or she shall also be blessed with status, fame and authority in life.

- Where only Jia Wood and Gui Water penetrate through the Heavenly Stems – with Gui (Yin) Water also denoted in one of the Earthly Branches – this Day Master shall be a cultured socialite, capable of interacting with virtually all levels of society.

- Where Bing Fire is revealed but Gui Water is not, this Day Master shall possess a genteel, learned disposition; although he or she may only lead an average life at best.

- Where only Earth Structures are formed in the BaZi Chart, this Day Master may be afflicted by loneliness, hardship and sadness in life.

- Where Earth is in abundance in the chart – and while Jia Wood penetrates through the Heavenly Stems, but Geng Metal is not revealed – this Day Master may succeed in life, although the extent of his or her success and influence would be limited.

| Day Master | Wu 戊 Earth | | Month | Wei 未 (Goat) |

Additional Attributes

Goat

格局 Structural Star	七殺 Seven Killings	正財 Direct Wealth	偏印 Indirect Resource
用神 Useful God	Jia 甲 Wood	Gui 癸 Water	Bing 丙 Fire
Conditions	Where Jia Wood, Gui Water and Bing Fire are all revealed in the Heavenly Stems, this Day Master shall enjoy superior success in his or her career-related pursuits. Even if Bing Fire were to be missing, this Day Master would still be a knowledgeable, learned person. Where Gui Water is missing, this Day Master may only lead an average, simple life at best.		
Positive Circumstances	Presence of Wood in the stems.		
Negative Circumstances	Where Jia Wood does not penetrate through the Heavenly Stems, this Day Master may be afflicted by poverty in life.		

Day Master	Wu 戊 Earth		Month	Wei 未 (Goat)

Additional Attributes

格局 Structural Star	七殺 Seven Killings
用神 Useful God	Jia 甲 Wood
Conditions	Where the Seven Killings Structure is formed and used, Geng Metal – an Eating God Star – should not be present to exert its control over Jia Wood.
Positive Circumstances	Presence of Ren Water in the chart.
Negative Circumstances	Geng Metal penetrates through the Heavenly Stems.

Goat

六月 Sixth Month

Day Master	Wu 戊 Earth	Month	Wei 未 (Goat)

Summary

- Where Jia Wood is missing, this Day Master may suffer from poor career and relationship luck, especially with regard to the relationship between male Day Masters and their wives.

- Without Water, the person may still be talented, but cash poor.

Goat

Wu 戊 Earth Day Master, Born in Seventh Month 七月

Shen 申 (Monkey) Month
August 8th - September 7th

Do note that the dates provided above are subject to slight yearly variations. Please refer to the Ten Thousand Year Calendar for the accurate transition dates for each year.

| Day Master | Wu 戊 Earth | | Month | Shen 申 (Monkey) |

七月 Seventh Month

Monkey

日元 Day Master	月 Month
戊 *Wu* **Yang Earth**	申 *Shen* **Monkey** **Yang Metal**

For a Wu Earth Day Master born in a Shen (Monkey) Month, an Eating God Structure is formed where Geng Metal is revealed as one of the Heavenly Stems.

Where Ren Water is revealed as one of the Heavenly Stems, an Indirect Wealth Structure is formed.

Where Wu Earth is revealed as one of the Heavenly Stems, the Thriving Structure is formed only when the strict conditions are met.

Should, however, neither Geng Metal, Ren Water or Wu Earth happen to be revealed amongst the Heavenly Stems, one should select a Structure according to the BaZi Chart's most prominent Qi attribute at one's discretion.

| Day Master | Wu 戊 Earth | Month | Shen 申 (Monkey) |

喜用神提要 **Regulating Useful God Reference Guide**

月 **Month**	用神 **Useful God**
7th Month 七月 **Shen 申 (Monkey) Month**	丙 *Bing* **Yang Fire** 癸 *Gui* **Yin Water** 甲 *Jia* **Yang Wood**

Monkey

For a Shen (Monkey) Month, Bing Fire, Gui Water and Jia Wood are the Regulating Useful Gods.

Since the Qi is becoming gradually colder this Month, Bing Fire is needed to provide 'warmth' for this Wu Earth Day Master.

Where Water is present in abundance, Jia Wood may be used to weaken and keep it under control.

BaZi Structures & Structural Useful Gods 格局與格局用神

Day Master	Wu 戊 Earth	Month	Shen 申 (Monkey)

8th day of August – 7th day of September, Gregorian Calendar

Geng Metal is at its strongest, in a Shen (Monkey) Month.

Water Qi is also considered to be strong this Month. Since the Qi is becoming gradually colder, Earth would be weakened where Water is present in abundance.

This is why Bing Fire is first needed to provide 'warmth' for this Day Master. Then and only then will this Day Master be a 'thick', 'solid' and hence, strong one, before Water may be play its role as a Useful God.

Where Earth is weak, Fire must invariably accompany the usage of Wood, as a Useful God. Indeed, it takes both to simultaneously support and strengthen this Day Master, and transform a weak Day Master into a stronger one. It is only under such circumstances that any wealth this Day Master generates or accumulates in life may be channeled towards productive or good usage.

A Wu Earth Day Master born in an hour when Fire and Earth happen to be strong would, however, enjoy comparatively better wealth luck than others.

| Day Master | Wu 戊 Earth | Month | Shen 申 (Monkey) |

Commentary

In addition to the preceding narratives on the potential Structures and scenarios resulting from a Wu Earth Day Master born in a Shen (Monkey) Month, the following circumstances also play their respective roles in determining the overall strength of this Day Master's BaZi Chart.

Note:

Monkey

- Bing Fire is the primary Useful God for a Wu Earth Day Master born in a Shen (Monkey) Month, with Gui Water and Jia Wood serving as secondary Useful Gods.

- Earth should never be parted from Jia Wood. Jia Wood is essential for the survival of Wu Earth.

- Only Water and Fire may be suitably employed as Regulating Useful Gods. Bing Fire and Gui Water play pivotal roles as 'Regulating' Useful Gods, in either 'warming up' or 'cooling down' the prevailing Qi, depending on the season of the year.

- Wu Earth forming a successful Eating God structure with the Geng Metal denotes and extremely talented and extraordinarily gifted person.

- Excessive Earth Qi denotes loneliness and sadness.

- Where Bing Fire, Jia Wood and Gui Water are missing from the Four Pillars of Destiny, the overall structure of this Day Master's BaZi Chart would still be a substandard one.

- The BaZi Chart would be of an ideal or favorable structure, where Bing Fire, Jia Wood and Gui Water are at least sufficiently present and used.

七月
Seventh Month

Monkey

| Day Master | Wu 戊 Earth | | Month | Shen 申 (Monkey) |

Additional Attributes

格局 Structural Star	偏印 Indirect Resource	正財 Direct Wealth	七殺 Seven Killings
用神 Useful God	Bing 丙 Fire	Gui 癸 Water	Jia 甲 Wood
Conditions	Where Bing Fire, Gui Water and Jia Wood are all rooted in their respective elements, this Day Master shall enjoy fame and success in life. Where only Bing Fire and Jia Wood are revealed, this Day Master shall still be a learned, knowledgeable one. Where only Gui Water and Jia Wood are revealed, this Day Master shall prosper and become wealthy in life.		
Positive Circumstances	Presence of Bing Fire, Gui Water and Jia Wood at the same time.		
Negative Circumstances	In the absence of Gui Water and Jia Wood, this Day Master may only lead an average life at best. Where Bing Fire and Jia Wood are missing, male Day Masters may end up getting married very late in life.		

| Day Master | Wu 戊 Earth | | Month | Shen 申 (Monkey) |

Additional Attributes

格局 Structural Star	偏財 Indirect Wealth	正財 Direct Wealth	食神 Eating God
用神 Useful God	Ren 壬 Water	Gui 癸 Water	Geng 庚 Metal
Conditions	Where the Earthly Branches form a Water Structure, Jia Wood (Seven Killings Star) may be used to weaken and keep Water under control. Geng Metal Eating God structure successfully formed. Presence of Jia Wood and Bing Fire – this person would be extraordinarily talented and gifted in artistic fields.		
Positive Circumstances	Jia Wood (a Seven Killings Star) is revealed in the Heavenly Stems.		
Negative Circumstances	Jia Wood is absent or missing from the BaZi Chart. Presence of too additional Earth may bring great fame but also grave loneliness and sadness.		

* Bing Fire, Gui Water and Jia Wood are the preferred Useful Gods for a Wu Earth Day Master born in a Shen (Monkey) Month.

七
月
Seventh Month

Monkey

Day Master	Wu 戊 Earth	Month	Shen 申 (Monkey)

Summary

- Where the Earthly Branches form a Water Structure, Bing Fire is needed to bring stability and calmness to pursue and achieve the many wealth goals in life.

Monkey

Wu 戊 Earth Day Master, Born in Eighth Month 八月

You 酉 (Rooster) Month
September 8th - October 7th

Do note that the dates provided above are subject to slight yearly variations. Please refer to the Ten Thousand Year Calendar for the accurate transition dates for each year.

BaZi Structures & Structural Useful Gods 格局與格局用神

| Day Master | Wu 戊 Earth | | Month | You 酉 (Rooster) |

日元 Day Master	月 Month
戊 *Wu* **Yang Earth**	酉 *You* **Rooster** **Yin Metal**

For a Wu Earth Day Master born in a You (Rooster) Month, a Hurting Officer Structure is formed where Xin Metal is revealed as one of the Heavenly Stems.

Even if Xin Metal is not revealed as a Hidden Stem, a Hurting Officer Structure would still be considered to have been formed.

| Day Master | Wu 戊 Earth | | Month | You 酉 (Rooster) |

喜用神提要 Regulating Useful God Reference Guide

Rooster

月 **Month**	用神 **Useful God**
8th Month 八月 **You 酉 (Rooster) Month**	丙 *Bing* **Yang Fire** 癸 *Gui* **Yin Water**

For a You (Rooster) Month, Bing Fire and Gui Water are the Regulating Useful Gods.

Much will depend on the ability of Bing Fire to provide 'warmth' to this Day Master, with Water to provide 'moisture' – if both are to play their respective roles as Useful Gods.

BaZi Structures & Structural Useful Gods 格局與格局用神

Day Master	Wu 戊 Earth	Month	You 酉 (Rooster)

8th day of September - 7th day of October, Gregorian Calendar

Metal is at its strongest this month.

Such strong Metal Qi would invariably weaken Earth. Unsurprisingly, it would be difficult for Wu Earth to 'contain' or 'harbor' anything. Without Bing Fire to produce and strengthen Earth, the latter will invariably be 'thick' but weak.

Excess Metal produces Water. And Water, in turn, has the potential to 'contaminate' and cause Earth to become 'messy' and 'muddy'.

Where Water exerts a counter-control over Earth, Earth would be weakened even more. Where Metal is present in abundance, this Day Master would be an intelligent, knowledgeable one – although he or she might find it harder to earn the recognition and appreciation due him or her.

The presence of Fire is crucial to the success of this person in life.

| Day Master | Wu 戊 Earth | Month | You 酉 (Rooster) |

Commentary

In addition to the preceding narratives on the potential Structures and scenarios resulting from a Wu Earth Day Master born in a You (Rooster) Month, the following circumstances also play their respective roles in determining the overall strength of this Day Master's BaZi Chart.

Note :

Rooster

- Bing Fire is the primary Useful God for a Wu Earth Day Master born in a You (Rooster) Month, with Gui Water as the secondary Useful God.

- Metal is extremely strong in a You (Rooster) Month. As such, it is capable of over 'loosening' and weakening Wu Earth. This is why it would be unnecessary to further use Jia Wood to 'loosen' Wu Earth.

- Bing Fire should hence be employed as the primary Useful God, to bring 'warmth' and stability to this Day Master. Where Bing Fire and Gui Water are both missing, this Day Master may lack a sense of purpose and direction in life.

- Where Bing Fire and Gui Water are revealed, this Day Master shall enjoy success in his or her career-related pursuits. The person would find happiness.

- Where Bing Fire is revealed but Gui Water remains hidden, this Day Master may only lead an average life, at best.

- Where Gui Water is revealed but Bing Fire remains hidden, this Day Master will still be able to lead a life of comfort or luxury. But may not be contented in life.

- Where Gui Water is revealed but Bing Fire is missing, this Day Master will possess a helpful, obliging personality. But life unfortunately seems to be always unfair towards him/her.

- Where Gui Water is present in abundance but - with Bing Fire - is not revealed, this Day Master may only lead an average life, at best.

- Where the Si (Snake), You (Rooster) and Chou (Ox) Earthly Branches form a Metal Structure, Bing Fire and Ding Fire should remain concealed as the Hidden Stems of the Earthly Branches – and should not be revealed in the Heavenly Stems. Otherwise, they would negate or neutralize the usefulness of the Metal Structure formed. If the circumstances are met, this Day Master shall be blessed with authority, status and fame in life.

- Where the Earthly Branches form a Water Structure – while Ren Water and Gui Water are also seen in the Heavenly Stems – this Day Master shall prosper and become wealthy in life.

- Where any Metal Qi present in the BaZi Chart is weakened considerably, this Day Master may be afflicted by poverty in life – no matter how hard he or she pretends to act otherwise. He or she will also tend to possess a moody disposition. Even if this Day Master prospers and enjoys wealth to a certain extent, his or her wealth would not be of use - and he or she may also be of a miserly disposition.

- Where there is no opportunity for Earth to be produced or strengthened, it is undesirable for Xin Metal to be seen penetrating through the Heavenly Stems and combining with Bing Fire to form Water.

- Amongst the Earthly Branches, Bing Fire and Ding Fire must at least be present as Hidden Stems.

Rooster

Day Master	Wu 戊 Earth		Month	You 酉 (Rooster)

Additional Attributes

格局 Structural Star	偏印 Indirect Resource	正財 Direct Wealth
用神 Useful God	Bing 丙 Fire	Gui 癸 Water
Conditions	Where both Bing Fire and Gui Water are revealed, this Day Master shall succeed tremendously in life. Even if Bing Fire and Gui Water are not revealed, this Day Master shall still be a learned, knowledgeable person albeit no success in life.	
Positive Circumstances	Bing Fire and Gui Water present in chart.	
Negative Circumstances	In the absence of Bing Fire and Gui Water, this Day Master may lack a sense of purpose and direction in life.	

格局 Structural Star	食神 Eating God	傷官 Hurting Officer
用神 Useful God	Geng 庚 Metal	Xin 辛 Metal
Conditions	Where Geng Metal and Xin Metal penetrate through the Heavenly Stems, Bing Fire and Ding Fire must also be revealed, in order to arrive at a best-case scenario for this Day Master.	
Positive Circumstances	Geng and Xin Metal both revealed in the Heavenly Stems	
Negative Circumstances	Excessive Earth elements in the chart.	

| Day Master | Wu 戊 Earth | | Month | You 酉 (Rooster) |

Additional Attributes

Rooster

格局 **Structural Star**	偏財 Indirect Wealth	正財 Direct Wealth
用神 **Useful God**	Ren 壬 Water	Gui 癸 Water
Conditions	Where the Earthly Branches form Water formation, this Day Master may be afflicted by poverty in life; regardless of how wealthy his or her family or household may be.	
Positive Circumstances	Companion Stars penetrate through Heavenly Stems.	
Negative Circumstances	Only Rob Wealth instead of Companion Stars are present.	

Bing Fire and Gui Water are the preferred Useful Gods for a Wu Earth Day Master born in a You (Rooster) Month.

| Day Master | Wu 戊 Earth | Month | You 酉 (Rooster) |

Summary

- Where only Xin Metal is present in the Heavenly Stems of this Day Master's BaZi Chart – with Bing Fire and Ding Fire conspicuously absent – the person lives a substandard life.

Wu 戊 Earth Day Master, Born in Ninth Month 九月

Xu 戌 (Dog) Month
October 8th - November 6th

Do note that the dates provided above are subject to slight yearly variations. Please refer to the Ten Thousand Year Calendar for the accurate transition dates for each year.

| Day Master | Wu 戊 Earth | Month | Xu 戌 (Dog) |

日元 Day Master	月 Month
戊 *Wu* **Yang Earth**	戌 *Xu* **Dog** **Yang Earth**

For a Wu Earth Day Master born in a Xu (Dog) Month, a Hurting Officer Structure is formed where Xin Metal is revealed as one of the Heavenly Stems.

Where Ding Fire is revealed as one of the Heavenly Stems, a Direct Resource Structure is formed.

Where Wu Earth is revealed as one of the Heavenly Stems, a Thriving Structure is formed when the conditions are supportive.

Should, however, neither Xin Metal, Ding Fire nor Wu Earth happen to be revealed amongst the Heavenly Stems, one should select a Structure according to the BaZi Chart's most prominent Qi attribute at one's discretion.

| Day Master | Wu 戊 Earth | | Month | Xu 戌 (Dog) |

喜用神提要 **Regulating Useful God Reference Guide**

月 **Month**	用神 **Useful God**
9th Month 九月 Xu 戌 **(Dog) Month**	甲 *Jia* **Yang Wood** 丙 *Bing* **Yang Fire** 癸 *Gui* **Yin Water**

Dog

For a Xu (Dog) Month, Jia Wood, Bing Fire and Gui Water are the Regulating Useful Gods.

Since Wu Earth is strongest this Month, Jia Wood should be employed as this Day Master's primary Useful God, with Bing Fire as the secondary Useful God.

Where Metal is seen, Gui Water should first be used; before Bing Fire is employed as an accompanying Useful God.

Day Master Wu 戊 Earth	Month Xu 戌 (Dog)

8th day of October – 6th day of November, Gregorian Calendar

In a Xu (Dog) Month, Earth is 'leaden' and 'thick'. This is why, this Day Master greatly depends on Wood as a Useful God to loosen the Earth. However, there is also a potential danger of becoming overly 'dry' or 'parched'. Hence Water is a necessary Useful God, in providing much-needed 'moisture'.

A Day Master born in an hour when Fire and Earth happen to be strong would prefer Metal and Water as Useful Gods, to Water and Wood. This is in order to prevent Earth, which is already 'thick'.

Dog

If Metal, Water and Wood are all available in the chart, the Qi flow would be smooth. Under such circumstances, this Day Master would surely prosper and become very wealthy and happy in life.

| Day Master | Wu 戊 Earth | | Month | Xu 戌 (Dog) |

Commentary

In addition to the preceding narratives on the potential Structures and scenarios resulting from a Wu Earth Day Master born in a Xu (Dog) Month, the following circumstances also play their respective roles in determining the overall strength of this Day Master's BaZi Chart.

Dog

Note:

- Jia Wood is the primary Useful God for a Wu Earth Day Master born in a Xu (Dog) Month, with Bing Fire and Gui Water serving as supporting and hence secondary Useful Gods.

- Where only Gui Water (Direct Wealth Star) is seen penetrating through the Heavenly Stems – and while Jia Wood and Bing Fire are not revealed in the Heavenly Stems – this Day Master may only lead an average life, at best.

- Where only Jia Wood is seen penetrating through the Heavenly Stems – and while Gui Water and Bing Fire are not revealed in the Heavenly Stems – this Day Master belongs to someone who would be a skillful and knowledgeable, but he or she may only lead an average life, at best. Success is only a dream.

- Where Bing Fire and Gui Water are amongst the Hidden Stems of the Earthly Branches – but Jia Wood is missing completely – this Day Master may only lead an average, mediocre life at best. He or she may also be afflicted by loneliness, lack of support and contentment in life.

- Where the Earthly Branches form a Water (Wealth) Structure, Companion Stars must be seen in the Heavenly Stems, in order to assist this Day Master. Then and only then may this Day Master prosper and become very wealthy in life.

- Where the Earthly Branches form a Fire Structure – and while Fire and Earth are both revealed in the Heavenly Stems – it would still be difficult for this 'parched' or 'dry' Wu Earth Day Master to 'flourish' in life. The absence of Water indicates that this Day Master may have to slog and struggle throughout his or her entire life.

Day Master	Wu 戊 Earth		Month	Xu 戌 (Dog)

Additional Attributes

格局 **Structural Star**	正財 Direct Wealth
用神 **Useful God**	Gui 癸 Water
Conditions	In the absence of Bing Fire and Jia Wood, Gui Water (Direct Wealth Star) may still give the necessary vitality to this BaZi Chart. Under such circumstances, this Day Master may still enjoy a modest level of fortune and success in life.
Positive Circumstances	-
Negative Circumstances	-

格局 **Structural Star**	七殺 Seven Killings
用神 **Useful God**	Jia 甲 Wood
Conditions	Where the Seven Killings Structure is formed – but Bing Fire and Gui Water are completely missing – this Day Master may struggle to achieve fame and fortune in life.
Positive Circumstances	Gui Water and Bing Fire are present.
Negative Circumstances	-

BaZi Structures & Structural Useful Gods 格局與格局用神

Day Master	Wu 戊 Earth	Month	Xu 戌 (Dog)

Additional Attributes

Dog

九月 Ninth Month

格局 Structural Star	偏財 Indirect Wealth	正財 Direct Wealth
用神 Useful God	Ren 壬 Water	Gui 癸 Water
Conditions	Where the Earthly Branches form a Water (Wealth) Structure, Wu Earth (Friend Star) must also be revealed, in order to provide support and noblemen help to the chart. With it, opportunities may be realized.	
Positive Circumstances	-	
Negative Circumstances	There is no Friend Star penetrating through the Heavenly Stems.	

格局 Structural Star	偏印 Indirect Resource	正印 Direct Resource
用神 Useful God	Bing 丙 Fire	Ding 丁 Fire
Conditions	Where the Earthly Branches form a Fire (Resource) Structure, Wealth and Officer Stars must also be revealed. Then and only then may this Day Master prosper and enjoy superior wealth luck in life.	
Positive Circumstances	Ren Water, Gui Water, Jia Wood and Yi Wood – as Wealth and Officer Stars – are simultaneously revealed in the Heavenly Stems.	
Negative Circumstances	Without Wood and Water (Wealth and Officer Stars), this Day Master may have to slog and struggle throughout his or her entire life.	

* Jia Wood and Gui Water are the primary Useful Gods for a Wu Earth Day Master born in a Xu (Dog) Month.

** Bing Fire serves as the secondary Useful God to this Day Master.

Day Master	Wu 戊 Earth	Month	Xu 戌 (Dog)

Summary

- Without Water in the BaZi Chart, the person may have to slog and struggle throughout their entire lives.

- The function of Wood is to loosen the hardened Earth.

- Friends star as opposed to Rob Wealth Stars are favorable when Water exceeds its limit.

- Rob Wealth Star present next to Wealth Stars would denote a lifetime of jealousy and emotional conflict.

Wu 戊 Earth Day Master, Born in Tenth Month 十月

Hai 亥 (Pig) Month
November 7th - December 6th

Do note that the dates provided above are subject to slight yearly variations. Please refer to the Ten Thousand Year Calendar for the accurate transition dates for each year.

| Day Master | Wu 戊 Earth | | Month | Hai 亥 (Pig) |

日元 Day Master	月 Month
戊 *Wu* **Yang Earth**	亥 *Hai* **Pig** **Yin Water**

For a Wu Earth Day Master born in a Pig (Hai) Month, an Indirect Wealth Structure is formed where Ren Water is revealed as one of the Heavenly Stems.

Where Jia Wood is revealed as one of the Heavenly Stems, a Seven Killings Structure is formed.

Should, however, neither Ren Water nor Jia Wood happen to be revealed amongst the Heavenly Stems, one should select a Structure according to the BaZi Chart's most prominent Qi attribute at one's discretion.

| Day Master | Wu 戊 Earth | Month | Hai 亥 (Pig) |

喜用神提要 Regulating Useful God Reference Guide

Pig

月 Month	用神 Useful God
10th Month 十月 **Hai 亥 (Pig) Month**	甲 *Jia* **Yang Wood** 丙 *Bing* **Yang Fire**

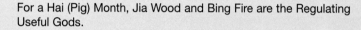

For a Hai (Pig) Month, Jia Wood and Bing Fire are the Regulating Useful Gods.

In any case, Jia Wood is indispensable as a Useful God to this Wu Earth Day Master.

Bing Fire plays an equally important role in providing 'warmth' to this Day Master.

十月 Tenth Month

亥
Pig

| Day Master | Wu 戊 Earth | | Month | Hai 亥 (Pig) |

7th day of November – 6th day of December, Gregorian Calendar

Water is extremely strong while Wood Qi is gaining momentum in a Hai (Pig) Month.

The time is early winter and the Qi would invariably tend to be cold, with Earth slowly weakening. And even though Wood may be 'moistened' by Water, which is strong in winter, it would still be difficult for Wood to produce Fire.

In fact, Wood and Fire will tend to weaken Water.

It would also be preferable for this Day Master to avoid meeting additional Metal Qi. This is because Metal controls Wood and produces Water, which would 'hurt' and weaken Wood and Fire, which are this Day Master's Useful Gods.

In any case, the wealth luck of a Wu Earth Day Master, born in an hour when Fire and Earth happen to be strong, shall invariably tend to be better.

Fire Qi helps bring vitality back to the Earth and is essential for healthy conditions.

Day Master	Wu 戊 Earth	Month	Hai 亥 (Pig)

Commentary

In addition to the preceding narratives on the potential Structures and scenarios resulting from a Wu Earth Day Master born in a Hai (Pig) Month, the following circumstances also play their respective roles in determining the overall strength of this Day Master's BaZi Chart.

Note:

- Bing Fire and Jia Wood are the preferred Useful Gods for a Wu Earth Day Master born in a Hai (Pig) Month.

- Bing Fire should be used to provide 'warmth' to a Wu Earth Day Master born in a winter month. Meanwhile, Jia Wood should be used to 'loosen' and 'plough' Earth.

- Where Bing Fire and Jia Wood are both revealed in the Heavenly Stems – while there is no Clash, Punishment or Harm Relationships taking place in the Earthly Branches– this Day Master shall enjoy success in his or her career-related pursuits.

- It is undesirable to have Geng Metal revealed in the Heavenly Stems. This is because Geng Metal has the potential to 'hurt' and 'destroy' Jia Wood, which is this Day Master's Useful God. And if this is the case, it would be difficult for this Day Master to achieve success in anything he or she does in life.

- Where neither Bing Fire nor Jia Wood is revealed in the Heavenly Stems – this Day Master may be afflicted by poverty and loneliness in life.

十月 Tenth Month

Pig

79

十
月

Tenth Month

亥
Pig

Day Master	Wu 戊 Earth		Month	Hai 亥 (Pig)

Additional Attributes

格局 **Structural Star**	七殺 Seven Killings	偏印 Indirect Resource
用神 **Useful God**	Jia 甲 Wood	Bing 丙 Fire
Conditions	Where Jia Wood and Bing Fire are both revealed, this Day Master shall enjoy success in his or her career-related pursuits.	
Positive Circumstances	Where Geng Metal is seen or encountered, Ding Fire must also accompany it.	
Negative Circumstances	Where Geng Metal (Eating God Star) penetrates through the Heavenly Stems, this Day Master may only lead an average life, at best.	

十月 Tenth Month

Day Master	Wu 戊 Earth	Month	Hai 亥 (Pig)

Additional Attributes

格局 **Structural Star**	偏財 Indirect Wealth
用神 **Useful God**	Ren 壬 Water
Conditions	Where Ren Water (Indirect Wealth Star) forms its respective structure in the BaZi Chart, Wu Earth (Friend Star) is needed to penetrate through the Heavenly Stems, in order for this Day Master to prosper in life.
Positive Circumstances	Wu Earth (a Friend Star) must not be missing from the BaZi Chart.
Negative Circumstances	Wu Earth (a Friend Star) is missing from the BaZi Chart.

Pig

* Jia Wood and Bing Fire are the preferred Useful Gods for a Wu Earth Day Master born in a Hai (Pig) Month.

十月 Tenth Month

亥 Pig

| Day Master | Wu 戊 Earth | Month | Hai 亥 (Pig) |

Summary

- Jia Wood and Bing Fire are preferred Useful Gods to a Wu Earth Day Master born in a Hai (Pig) Month. Even if neither penetrates through the Heavenly Stems, their presence would at least bring about favorable outcomes to this person.

- It is undesirable to have Geng Metal and Ren Water in the Heavenly Stems. These stars would be 'hurting' the needed Jia Wood and insulting the important Bing Fire, which are this Day Master's Useful Gods.

- In the absence of Bing Fire, this Day Master may be afflicted by loneliness, lack of contentment in life.

- Where Geng Metal penetrates through the Heavenly Stems, Ding Fire must also be seen. Where Ren Water penetrates through the Heavenly Stems, Wu Earth (a Friend Star) must also be seen penetrating through the Heavenly Stems.

Wu 戊 Earth Day Master, Born in Eleventh Month 十一月

Zi 子 (Rat) Month
December 7th - January 5th

Do note that the dates provided above are subject to slight yearly variations. Please refer to the Ten Thousand Year Calendar for the accurate transition dates for each year.

Day Master	Wu 戊 Earth	Month	Zi 子 (Rat)

十一月
Eleventh Month

Rat

日元 Day Master	月 Month
戊 *Wu* **Yang Earth**	子 *Zi* **Rat** **Yang Water**

For a Wu Earth Day Master born in a Zi (Rat) Month, a Direct Wealth Structure is formed where Gui Water is revealed as one of the Heavenly Stems.

Even if Gui Water is not revealed as a Heavenly Stem, a Direct Wealth Structure would still be considered to have been formed.

| Day Master | Wu 戊 Earth | Month | Zi 子 (Rat) |

喜用神提要 Regulating Useful God Reference Guide

月 Month	用神 Useful God	
11th Month 十一月 Zi 子 (Rat) Month	丙 *Bing* **Yang Fire**	甲 *Jia* **Yang Wood**

Rat

For a Zi (Rat) Month, Bing Fire and Jia Wood are the Regulating Useful Gods.

Bing Fire is the primary Useful God to this Day Master, with Jia Wood serving as a secondary Useful God.

| **Day Master** | Wu 戊 Earth | **Month** | Zi 子 (Rat) |

7th day of December – 5th day of January, Gregorian Calendar

Given the mid winter timing of a Wu Earth Day Master's birth, his or her BaZi Chart's Qi would invariably tend to be extremely cold.

As such, Fire would be needed to bring 'warmth' to this Day Master. Only the 'hot' or 'warmed' Earth would be able to support the growth of ten thousand things. Without warmth, life is filled with emptiness.

Dry wood Wood may be also used to weaken the excessive Water, which is strong in winter. Dry Wood – i.e. Wood that harbors Fire Qi within it – will ensure the continuity of Fire Qi.

Fire that is not rooted or positioned in Sheng (Growth) would be useless to this Day Master.

It is undesirable for this Day Master to meet additional Metal and Water Qi. Otherwise, this Day Master may be afflicted by poor health in life, despite of how wealthy he or she may become.

Meeting Rob Wealth star with exposed Ren Water denotes that any appearances he or she may assume would be 'muddied' or deceiving, since it is likelt that this Day Master may still be personally poor; no matter how wealthy his or her household may be.

| Day Master | Wu 戊 Earth | Month | Zi 子 (Rat) |

Commentary

Rat

In addition to the preceding narratives on the potential Structures and scenarios resulting from a Wu Earth Day Master born in a Zi (Rat) Month, the following circumstances also play their respective roles in determining the overall strength of this Day Master's BaZi Chart.

Note:

- Bing Fire is the primary Useful God for a Wu Earth Day Master born in a Zi (Rat) Month, with Jia Wood serving as its secondary Useful God.

- Without Bing Fire (or at the very least, Ding Fire), any structure that is formed would be deemed substandard.

- Since Wu Earth is extremely cold or even frozen at this time of the year, it would be impossible for it to produce anything. And this is why Wu Earth remains under the mercy of Jia Wood.

- Where Ren Water and Gui Water are seen in the Heavenly Stems, a Follow the Wealth Structure may be formed in the BaZi Chart when the overall conditions supports it. Where the structure is successful, the person may lead an extraordinary life.

- Where a Gui Water (Direct Wealth Star) are present in the Month or Hour Pillars of the BaZi Chart, it would seek to combine with the Wu Earth to form Fire. However, such combination's success much depends on the Earthly Branches' conditions. A Day Master with such a scenario would be able to generate and accumulate wealth; although his or her wealth would usually be extremely hard-earned. Sometimes even through life risking endeavours.

- It is undesirable to have Xin Metal revealed in the Heavenly Stems. This is because Xin metal combines with Bing Fire. Where this happens, this person may find it extremely difficult to attain a sense of peace and harmony in life.

- Where there is an abundance of Bing Fire revealed in the Heavenly Stems, this Day Master may be inclined towards living an overly simple and humble life; perhaps one akin to that of a monk or hermit. He or she may be incapable of truly appreciating and enjoying life to the fullest. Under such circumstances, at least one Ren Water element must be revealed, if this Day Master is to at least enjoy a minimal level of material existence in life.

- Where Bing Fire is completely missing from the chart, Ji Earth may be used to replace it. Under such circumstances, this Day Master shall enjoy good 'people' or relationship luck, although he or she may not really be wealthy or prosperous in life.

- Where Geng Metal and Xin Metal are revealed in the chart, this person may enjoy unexpected status, power and authority in life. However, it the person's life 'fails' in success. Meaning, the more successful he/she becomes, the more pain and empty he or she feels.

Day Master	Wu 戊 Earth	Month	Zi 子 (Rat)

Additional Attributes

格局 Structural Star	偏印 Indirect Resource	七殺 Seven Killings
用神 Useful God	Bing 丙 Fire	Jia 甲 Wood
Conditions	Where Bing Fire and one Jia Wood elements are all revealed in the Heavenly Stems, this Day Master shall succeed in his or her life's pursuits.	
Positive Circumstances	Both Bing Fire and Jia Wood are present.	
Negative Circumstances	Where Bing Fire and Jia Wood are completely missing, the overall structure of the BaZi Chart would be a substandard one.	

格局 Structural Star	偏印 Indirect Resource
用神 Useful God	Bing 丙 Fire
Conditions	Where the Earthly Branches form a Fire (Resource) Structure, at least one Ren Water element should be revealed in the Heavenly Stems. If this is seen, this Day Master shall be inclined towards leading a simple, humble life, regardless of how wealthy he or she may become.
Positive Circumstances	Ren Water penetrates through the Heavenly Stems.
Negative Circumstances	Without Ren Water penetrating through the Heavenly Stems, this Day Master may be afflicted by loneliness and solitariness in life.

| Day Master | Wu 戊 Earth | Month | Zi 子 (Rat) |

Additional Attributes

格局 Structural Star	偏財 Indirect Wealth	正財 Direct Wealth
用神 Useful God	Ren 壬 Water	Gui 癸 Water
Conditions	Where Bing Fire is seen this person may enjoy an easy path to wealth. Where two Gui Water elements compete to combine with Wu Earth to form Fire, this Day Master may have to slog and struggle to achieve success in life.	
Positive Circumstances	Bing Fire must also be seen in the BaZi Chart.	
Negative Circumstances	Companion (i.e. Friend and Rob Wealth) Stars are seen .	

Rat

* Bing Fire and Jia Wood are the preferred Useful Gods for a Wu Earth Day Master born in a Zi (Rat).

| Day Master | Wu 戊 Earth | Month | Zi 子 (Rat) |

Summary

十一月

Eleventh Month

Rat

- Without Bing Fire all structures formed are substandard.

- Where Companion – i.e. Friend and Rob Wealth – Stars are present in overabundance, and while Earth Qi is also abundantly present in the Earthly Branches, only Jia Wood (Seven Killings Star) may be suitably employed as a preferred Useful God.

- Wood helps bring vitality back to the Earth. This is reverse growth.

Wu 戊 Earth Day Master, Born in Twelfth Month 十二月

Chou 丑 (Ox) Month
January 6th - February 3rd

Do note that the dates provided above are subject to slight yearly variations. Please refer to the Ten Thousand Year Calendar for the accurate transition dates for each year.

| Day Master | Wu 戊 Earth | Month | Chou 丑 (Ox) |

日元 Day Master	月 Month
戊 *Wu* **Yang Earth**	丑 *Chou* **Ox** **Yin Earth**

For a Wu Earth Day Master born in a Chou (Ox) Month, an Indirect Wealth Structure is formed where Gui Water is revealed as one of the Heavenly Stems.

Where Xin Metal is revealed as one of the Heavenly Stems, a Hurting Officer Structure is formed.

Where Ji Earth is revealed as one of the Heavenly Stems, a Goat Blade Structure is formed when the conditions are supportive.

Should, however, neither Xin Metal, Gui Water nor Ji Earth happen to be revealed within the Heavenly Stems, one should select the BaZi Chart's most prominent Qi attribute at one's discretion.

| Day Master | Wu 戊 Earth | Month | Chou 丑 (Ox) |

喜用神提要 **Regulating Useful God Reference Guide**

月 Month	用神 Useful God
12th Month 十二月 Chou 丑 (Ox) Month	丙 *Bing* **Yang Fire**　　　甲 *Jia* **Yang Wood**

Ox

For a Chou (Ox) Month, Bing Fire and Jia Wood are the Regulating Useful Gods.

Bing Fire is the primary Useful God to this Day Master, with Jia Wood serving as a secondary Useful God.

Day Master Wu 戊 Earth   **Month Chou 丑 (Ox)**

6th day of January – 3rd day of February, Gregorian Calendar

Earth, in a Chou (Ox) Month would invariably tend to be cold and also 'icy' given that Water (or Snow) is strong in winter. Earth would be incapable of producing anything, given the freezing circumstances brought about by this month.

Warmth and heat are hence greatly preferred by this Day Master, in order for Earth to produce anything. As such, Fire serves as the Regulating Useful God for this Day Master.

A Chou (Ox) Month also stores hidden Metal Qi. As such, inorder for Wood to be used effectively, Wood needs to that harbor some Fire Qi within it. Only with the combination of Wood and Fire Qi, would be capable of aiding the other elements in bringing balance to this Day Master.

It is undesirable for this Day Master to meet additional Metal and Water Qi.

This is because Fire Qi may be 'hurt' or weakened with Metal and Water Qi. These elements would cause the overall Qi of the chart to become even colder.

| Day Master | Wu 戊 Earth | Month | Chou 丑 (Ox) |

Commentary

In addition to the preceding narratives on the potential Structures and scenarios resulting from a Wu Earth Day Master born in a Chou (Ox) Month, the following circumstances also play their respective roles in determining the overall strength of this Day Master's BaZi Chart.

Note:

- Bing Fire is the primary Useful God for a Wu Earth Day Master born this Month, with Jia Wood as the secondary Useful God.

- Without Bing Fire, all structures formed would only be sub pared.

- It is undesirable to have Xin Metal revealed in the Heavenly Stems. It is even more undesirable for the Earthly Branches to form a Metal Structure. This is because Xin Metal combines with Bing Fire, the Useful God. If this is seen, the Day Master may find life to be cold, unhappy and miserable, despite the person being highly talented.

Day Master	Wu 戊 Earth	Month	Chou 丑 (Ox)

Additional Attributes

格局 **Structural Star**	偏印 Indirect Resource	七殺 Seven Killings
用神 **Useful God**	Bing 丙 Fire	Jia 甲 Wood
Conditions	Where two Bing Fire and one Jia Wood elements are all revealed in the Heavenly Stems, this Day Master shall enjoy great succees in his or her life's pursuits.	
Positive Circumstances	Bing Fire and Jia Wood present in the chart.	
Negative Circumstances	Where Bing Fire and Jia Wood are completely missing, the overall structure of the BaZi Chart would be a substandard one.	

格局 **Structural Star**	偏印 Indirect Resource
用神 **Useful God**	Bing 丙 Fire
Conditions	Where the Earthly Branches form a Fire (Resource) Structure, at least one Ren Water element should be revealed in the Heavenly Stems. If this is seen, this Day Master shall be inclined towards leading a simple, humble life, regardless of how wealthy he or she may become.
Positive Circumstances	Ren Water penetrates through the Heavenly Stems. Absence of Xin Metal.
Negative Circumstances	Without Ren Water penetrating through the Heavenly Stems, this Day Master may be afflicted by loneliness in life. It would be even worse if Xin Metal is found next to the Bing Fire.

Day Master	Wu 戊 Earth		Month	Chou 丑 (Ox)

Additional Attributes

格局 Structural Star	偏財 Indirect Wealth	正財 Direct Wealth
用神 Useful God	Ren 壬 Water	Gui 癸 Water
Conditions	Bing Fire and Ren Water makes a powerful configuration.	
Positive Circumstances	Presenc of Bing Fire.	
Negative Circumstances	Companion (Friend and Rob Wealth) Stars are seen.	

* *Bing Fire and Jia Wood are the preferred Useful Gods for a Wu Earth Day Master born in a Chou (Ox) Month.*

十二月 Twelfth Month

丑
Ox

97

| Day Master | Wu 戊 Earth | Month | Chou 丑 (Ox) |

Summary

- Without Bing Fire there would be lack of quality in the BaZi Chart.

- Jia Wood is necessary to keep the Earth's vitality and to support the growth of Fire.

Ji (己) Earth Day Master

Overview:

Ji 己 Earth is Yin Earth. It can be represented or depicted as the sands found on the beach or seaside, or the moist and wet earth commonly found in the garden. Being Earth, it is rather receptive and tolerant of varying circumstances. In fact, Ji Earth has a very high level of tolerance, regardless of the circumstances surrounding it.

Meanwhile, its Yin nature also allows Ji Earth to be soft and even yielding and pliant, if necessary. Unsurprisingly, it would also be unsuitable for Ji Earth to encounter Water – especially large or powerful bodies of Water – as well as strong Wood. Strong or powerful Metal also has the potential to weaken it, and hence be avoided as well.

As one should be able to surmise by now, Ji Earth Day Masters are productive, tolerant and resourceful. They also tend to be more understanding of the weaknesses and fallacies of others.

Ji Earth types, however, lack the ability to make quick, spontaneous decisions when needed – due to their lack of adaptability. They are, however, relatively gentler, more yielding and receptive in nature, compared to their Wu Earth counterparts – due to Ji Earth's Yin nature.

Ji 己 Earth Day Master, Born in First Month 正月

Yin 寅 (Tiger) Month
February 4th – March 5th

Do note that the dates provided above are subject to slight yearly variations. Please refer to the Ten Thousand Year Calendar for the accurate transition dates for each year.

| Day Master Ji 己 Earth | Month Yin 寅 (Tiger) |

日元 Day Master	月 Month
己 Ji Yin Earth	寅 Yin Tiger Yang Wood

For a Ji Earth Day Master born in a Yin (Tiger) Month, a Direct Officer Structure is formed where Jia Wood is revealed as one of the Heavenly Stems.

Where Bing Fire is revealed as one of the Heavenly Stems, a Direct Resource Structure is formed.

Where Wu Earth is revealed as one of the Heavenly Stems, a Goat Blade Structure may be formed when the overall conditions are supportive.

Should, however, neither Jia Wood, Bing Fire nor Wu Earth happen to be revealed within the Heavenly Stems, one should select the BaZi Chart's most prominent Qi attribute at one's discretion.

| Day Master | Ji 己 Earth | Month | Yin 寅 (Tiger) |

喜用神提要 Regulating Useful God Reference Guide

月 Month	用神 Useful God
1st Month 正月 Yin 寅 (Tiger) Month	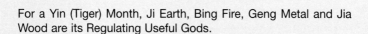 丙 *Bing* **Yang Fire** 庚 *Geng* **Yang Metal** 甲 *Jia* **Yang Wood**

Tiger

For a Yin (Tiger) Month, Ji Earth, Bing Fire, Geng Metal and Jia Wood are its Regulating Useful Gods.

Bing Fire should be used to bring some warmth to an otherwise 'cold' or 'chilly' Ji Earth Day Master born in a Yin (Tiger) Month.

It is undesirable to be encountering Ren Water for this chart.

Where Water is present in abundance, Wu Earth may be used as an intermediary Useful God, in keeping Water under control. Likewise, where Earth is present in abundance, Jia Wood may be used to keep Earth under control. Similarly, where Jia Wood is present in abundance, Geng Metal may be used to keep Jia Wood under control.

BaZi Structures & Structural Useful Gods 格局與格局用神

Day Master	Ji 己 Earth	Month	Yin 寅 (Tiger)

4th day of February – 5th day of March, Gregorian Calendar

For a Ji Earth Day Master born in a Yin (Tiger) Month, Jia Wood, Bing Fire and Wu Earth all play their respective roles as Useful Gods; ranging from bringing warmth to balancing and supporting each other in ensuring vitality of the Earth.

Fire Qi is needed to bring warmth and inject some 'life' into this otherwise cold scenario.

Tiger

Where Fire and Earth Qi happen to be strong in the chart, Metal and Water stars would then play their roles as Useful Gods, in bringing balance to this Day Master's BaZi Chart, and ensuring that it remains sentimental and obviously, well-balanced.

Day Master	Ji 己 Earth		Month	Yin 寅 (Tiger)

Commentary

Tiger

In addition to the preceding narratives on the potential Structures and scenarios resulting from a Ji Earth Day Master born in a Yin (Tiger) Month, the following circumstances also play their respective roles in determining the overall strength of this Day Master's BaZi Chart.

Note:

- Bing Fire is the primary Useful God, with Jia Wood and Gui Water serving as the secondary Useful Gods to a Ji Earth Day Master born in a Yin (Tiger) Month.

- It is undesirable for Ren Water to be seen penetrating through the Heavenly Stems.

- Jia Wood is needed to 'loosen' Ji Earth right after the frost in Winter. Ji Earth, however, should avoid encountering Ren Water; although not Gui Water. Ren Water denotes flooding at this time of the month.

- Regardless of whether Jia Wood is present in the Heavenly Stems or Hidden Stems of the Earthly Branches, Geng Metal must be present, followed by Bing Fire and Gui Water. Where all three Useful Gods are present, this Ji Earth Day Master shall enjoy a great life of prosperity and happiness.

- Where Jia Wood is present in abundance but Geng Metal is missing, this Ji Earth Day Master may be inclined towards possessing an indolent or idle personality.

- Where the Earthly Branches forms a Fire Structure, coupled with the absence of Ren Water, this Ji Earth Day Master shall enjoy great prosperity in life. (Since Ji Earth is already considered 'wet' or 'moist' Earth, it would not be necessary for Ren Water to be revealed.)

- Even though Yi Wood may be revealed in the Heavenly Stems, Yi Wood simply cannot 'loosen' or bring balance to this Ji Earth Day Master. Under such circumstances, this Ji Earth Day Master may not be able to match his or her actions with words uttered, or promises given.

Day Master	Ji 己 Earth	Month	Yin 寅 (Tiger)

Additional Attributes

Tiger

格局 **Structural Star**	正官 Direct Officer
用神 **Useful God**	Jia 甲 Wood
Conditions	Where the Earthly Branches form a Wood (Seven Killings Star) Structure, Geng Metal - the Hurting Officer Star - would be needed to penetrate through the Heavenly Stems.
Positive Circumstances	Geng Metal – Hurting Officer Star – penetrates through the Heavenly Stems. Xin Metal – an Eating God Star – would however be useless.
Negative Circumstances	There is no Metal to penetrate through the Heavenly Stems.

格局 **Structural Star**	正印 Direct Resource
用神 **Useful God**	Bing 丙 Fire
Conditions	Where the Earthly Branches form a Fire (Resource Star) Structure, even though Water may be absent from the Four Pillars of Destiny, this Ji Earth Day Master would still fare quite well.
Positive Circumstances	Presence of Gui Water in the chart.
Negative Circumstances	Wu Earth – Rob Wealth Star – should be prevented from penetrating through the Heavenly Stems.

| Day Master | Ji 己 Earth | Month | Yin 寅 (Tiger) |

Additional Attributes

格局 **Structural Star**	七殺 Seven Killings
用神 **Useful God**	Yi 乙 Wood
Conditions	Where a Seven Killings Structure is formed, this Ji Earth Day Master shall possess a gentle yet intelligent personality.
Positive Circumstances	Presence of Gui Water.
Negative Circumstances	Absense of Geng Metal next to Yi Wood.

* Bing Fire is the primary Useful God for a Ji Earth Day Master born in a Yin (Tiger) Month.

**Jia Wood and Gui Water are the secondary Useful Gods.

正月 **First Month**

Tiger

| Day Master | Ji 己 Earth | Month | Yin 寅 (Tiger) |

Summary

- Where Water – Wealth Star - is missing from the chart, this Day Master would still fare quite well. This is because Ji Earth is considered wet earth.

- Yi Wood – Seven Killings Star – is unable to loosen the Earth effectively this month.

Tiger

Ji 己 Earth Day Master, Born in Second Month 二月

Mao 卯 (Rabbit) Month
March 6th – April 4th

Do note that the dates provided above are subject to slight yearly variations. Please refer to the Ten Thousand Year Calendar for the accurate transition dates for each year.

| Day Master | Ji 己 Earth | Month | Mao 卯 (Rabbit) |

日元 Day Master	月 Month
己 Ji Yin Earth	卯 Mao Rabbit Yin Wood

For a Ji Earth Day Master born in a Mao (Rabbit) Month, a Seven Killings Structure is formed where Yi Wood is revealed as one of the Heavenly Stems.

Even if Yi Wood is not revealed as a Heavenly Stem, a Seven Killings Structure would still be considered to have been formed.

| Day Master | Ji 己 Earth | | Month | Mao 卯 (Rabbit) |

喜用神提要 **Regulating Useful God Reference Guide**

二月 Second Month

卯 Rabbit

月 **Month**	用神 **Useful God**
2nd Month 二月 Mao 卯 (Rabbit) Month	甲 *Jia* **Yang Wood**　　癸 *Gui* **Yin Water**　　丙 *Bing* **Yang Fire**

For a Mao (Rabbit) Month, Jia Wood, Gui Water and Bing Fire are its Regulating Useful Gods.

Jia Wood is the primary Useful God for a Ji Earth Day Master born in a Mao (Rabbit) Month. Ji Earth however, should be prevented from combining with Jia Wood and transforming into Earth.

Meanwhile, Gui Water may be used as a secondary Useful God to 'moisten' this Ji Earth Day Master.

Day Master	Ji 己 Earth	Month	Mao 卯 (Rabbit)

6th day of March – 4th day of April, Gregorian Calendar

Since a Mao (Rabbit) Month denotes the mid of spring season, Wood Qi is at its peak.

As such, Wood Qi would invariably control Ji Earth. Ji Earth would be lacking the strength necessary to combine with Jia Wood.

Since wood Qi is at its peak Fire would be needed to weaken the Wood so that it does not become a Sha 煞 or Negative Qi to this Ji Earth Day Master. In addition, Fire can also serve as a favorable Resource Star to produce and strengthen this Day Master.

Fire Qi is preferred over Metal, as a Useful God in bringing balance to this Ji Earth Day Master. This is because Metal weakens Earth while Fire strengthens.

Where Fire and Earth are particularly strong, Water should be chosen as Useful God. This is obvious, since Water will moderate and keep Fire under control, and therefore prevent the overall environment of this Chart from becoming overly 'hot'.

二月 Second Month

卯 Rabbit

Day Master	Ji 己 Earth		Month	Mao 卯 (Rabbit)

Commentary

In addition to the preceding narratives on the potential Structures and scenarios resulting from a Ji Earth Day Master born in a Mao (Rabbit) Month, the following circumstances also play their respective roles in determining the overall strength of this Day Master's BaZi Chart.

Note:

- Jia Wood and Bing Fire are the preferred Useful Gods for a Ji Earth Day Master born in a Mao (Rabbit) Month, with Gui Water serving as the secondary Useful God.

- Ji Earth and Jia Wood should be prevented from combining with one another.

- Where a complete Wood formation is seen in the Earthly branches, Geng Metal is essential for survival of the chart. (In the absence of Geng Metal, Ding Fire may be used instead. This is because Ding Fire weakens Jia Wood, which is another Useful God for this Ji Earth Day Master. However, this format would indicate that this person might harbor insidious motives and hidden agenda.)

- Where Jia Wood, Gui Water and Bing Fire are missing from the Heavenly Stems, this Ji Earth Day Master may only lead an average life, at best.

- Where Ren Water and Ji Earth are both revealed in the Heavenly Stems, this Ji Earth Day Master's career-related prospects may not be too promising.

二月 Second Month

Rabbit

| Day Master | Ji 己 Earth | Month | Mao 卯 (Rabbit) |

Additional Attributes

Rabbit

格局 **Structural Star**	正官 Direct Officer	偏財 Indirect Wealth
用神 **Useful God**	Jia 甲 Wood	Gui 癸 Water
Conditions	With Jia Wood (Direct Officer Star) is present, this Ji Earth Day Master shall succeed in his or her career-related endeavors. The best-case scenario would be for Jia Wood to be found in the Heavenly Stem of the Year Pillar.	
Positive Circumstances	Bing Fire is present in the chart.	
Negative Circumstances	Jia Wood and this Ji Earth Day Master are found side-by-side in the BaZi Chart, while Geng Metal also penetrates through the Heavenly Stems and has Jia Wood under its control.	

二月 Second Month

Day Master	Ji 己 Earth	Month	Mao 卯 (Rabbit)

Additional Attributes

格局 **Structural Star**	正官 Direct Officer	七殺 Seven Killings
用神 **Useful God**	Jia 甲 Wood	Yi 乙 Wood
Conditions	Where the Earthly Branches form a Wood (Seven Killings Star) Structure, Geng Metal (Hurting Officer Star) would be needed to penetrate through the Heavenly Stems.	
Positive Circumstances	Where there is no Geng Metal to penetrate through the Heavenly Stems, Ding Fire may be used to weaken Jia Wood.	
Negative Circumstances	Yi Wood – theSeven Killings Star – penetrates through the Heavenly Stems and combines with Geng Metal – the Hurting Officer Star.	

Rabbit

* Jia Wood, Bing Fire and Gui Water are the preferred Useful Gods for a Ji Earth Day Master born in a Mao (Rabbit) Month.

**Jia Wood – the Direct Officer Star – should be prevented from combining with this Ji Earth Day Master.

Day Master	Ji 己 Earth		Month	Mao 卯 (Rabbit)

Summary

- Absence of Bing Fire denotes lack of satisfaction in life.

- Jia Wood and Gui Water – as Useful Gods – should not be 'trapped'.

- Where Geng Metal, Ren Water and Wu Earth happen to be present in abundance, however, this Ji Earth Day Master may only lead an average life, at best.

- Where the Earthly Branches form Wood formation, without any Resource or Companion Stars present, a Follow the Killings Structure may be formed.

- Where Bing Fire, Jia Wood and Gui Water are completely absent from the chart, any structure formed would still be a substandard one.

二月 Second Month

Rabbit

Ji 己 Earth Day Master, Born in Third Month 三月

Chen 辰 (Dragon) Month
April 5th - May 5th

Do note that the dates provided above are subject to slight yearly variations. Please refer to the Ten Thousand Year Calendar for the accurate transition dates for each year.

Day Master Ji 己 Earth		**Month** Chen 辰 (Dragon)

日元 **Day Master**	月 **Month**
己 *Ji* **Yin Earth**	辰 *Chen* **Dragon** **Yang Earth**

For a Ji Earth Day Master born in a Chen (Dragon) Month, a Seven Killings Structure is formed where Yi Wood is revealed as one of the Heavenly Stems.

Where Gui Water is revealed as one of the Heavenly Stems, an Indirect Wealth Structure is formed.

Where Wu Earth is revealed as one of the Heavenly Stems, a possible Goat Blade Structure may be formed depending on the conditions of the chart.

Should, however, neither Yi Wood, Gui Water nor Wu Earth happen to be revealed within the Heavenly Stems, one should select a Structure according to the BaZi Chart's most prominent Qi attribute at one's discretion.

Day Master Ji 己 Earth   **Month** Chen 辰 (Dragon)

喜用神提要 Regulating Useful God Reference Guide

月 Month	用神 Useful God
3rd Month 三月 Chen 辰 (Dragon) Month	丙 *Bing* **Yang Fire** 癸 *Gui* **Yin Water** 甲 *Jia* **Yang Wood**

辰
Dragon

For a Chen (Dragon) Month, Bing Fire, Gui Water and Jia Wood are its most important Regulating Useful Gods.

Bing Fire is the primary Useful God for a Ji Earth Day Master born in a Chen (Dragon) Month, with Gui Water serving as the secondary Useful God.

Since Earth tends to be 'warm' and 'moist' in a Chen (Dragon) Month, Jia Wood should be used to 'loosen' and ensure that Earth Qi remains well-balanced.

Day Master	Ji 己 Earth	Month	Chen 辰 (Dragon)

5th day of April – 5th day of May, Gregorian Calendar

The Chen (Dragon) Earthly Branch – contains the Hidden Stems of Wu Earth, Yi Wood and Gui Water. Earth Qi would also be prominent in a Chen (Dragon) Month.

Water is necessary to keep the vitality of the Earth in this month. Where the Ji Earth Day Master meets with at least a reasonable amount of Water in the chart, the person shall enjoy prosperity in life. Where both Water and Wood Qi are appropriately located, this person shall enjoy fame, status and authority in life.

Where Fire and Earth Qi happen to be strong in the chart, Metal and Water are needed as Useful Gods.

Where Metal and Water Qi happen to be strong, Fire and Earth would then have to be used as 'arbitrating' Useful Gods, in order to 'adjust' the overall Qi of this Day Master's BaZi Chart.

Dragon

三月 Third Month

120

| Day Master | Ji 己 Earth | | Month | Chen 辰 (Dragon) |

Commentary

In addition to the preceding narratives on the potential Structures and scenarios resulting from a Ji Earth Day Master born in a Chen (Dragon) Month, the following circumstances also play their respective roles in determining the overall strength of this Day Master's BaZi Chart.

Note:

- Bing Fire is the primary Useful God for a Ji Earth Day Master born in a Chen (Dragon) Month, while Gui Water serves as the secondary Useful God, and Jia Wood as the tertiary Useful God.

- Jia Wood is needed in order to 'loosen' the Earth.

- Ji Earth has the propensity to 'store' Water, due to its Yin nature.

- Where Bing Fire, Jia Wood and Gui Water are revealed in the Chart, this Ji Earth Day Master shall enjoy an excellent quality of life.

- Where Yi Wood is revealed in the Heavenly Stems and Earthly Branches – but Geng Metal is missing– Earth Qi and Wood Qi may find themselves at conflicting odds with one another. Under such circumstances, this Ji Earth Day Master may be afflicted by poverty, as well as poor health throughout his or her entire life.

- Where Bing Fire is revealed – but Gui Water is not – this Ji Earth Day Master may prosper or accumulate wealth in small quantities in life; although he or she may never become immensely wealthy.

- Where Gui Water is revealed – but Bing Fire and Jia Wood are not – this Ji Earth Day Master may only lead an average life, at best.

- Where Bing Fire and Gui Water are revealed – but Jia Wood is not – this Ji Earth Day Master would at least possess the requisite skills and knowledge to succeed in life.

Dragon

三月 Third Month

辰 Dragon

Day Master Ji 己 Earth		**Month** Chen 辰 (Dragon)	

Additional Attributes

格局 **Structural Star**	正印 Direct Resource	偏財 Indirect Wealth	正官 Direct Officer
用神 **Useful God**	Bing 丙 Fire	Gui 癸 Water	Jia 甲 Wood
Conditions	Where Bing Fire, Gui Water and Jia Wood are all revealed, this Ji Earth Day Master shall certainly prosper in life. Where only one of the three is revealed, however, this Ji Earth Day Master may lack a sense of purpose or control over his or her life; although he or she shall still prosper in life.		
Positive Circumstances	All three – Bing Fire, Gui Water and Jia Wood present.		
Negative Circumstances	Bing Fire is used, but Ren Water is next to it. Where Gui Water is used, but Ji Earth is next to it. Where Jia Wood is used, but Geng Metal is right next to it.		

| Day Master | Ji 己 Earth | Month | Chen 辰 (Dragon) |

三月 Third Month

Additional Attributes

格局 **Structural Star**	七殺 Seven Killings
用神 **Useful God**	Yi 乙 Wood
Conditions	Where the Earthly Branches form a Wood formation (Seven Killings Star) - without Metal to keep Wood under control – this Ji Earth Day Master may not be blessed with longevity.
Positive Circumstances	Metal penetrates through the Heavenly Stems.
Negative Circumstances	Where Metal is missing from the chart, any structure formed will be substandard.

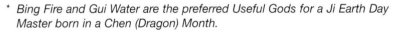

Dragon

*   *Bing Fire and Gui Water are the preferred Useful Gods for a Ji Earth Day Master born in a Chen (Dragon) Month.*

***Jia Wood is the secondary Useful God.*

Day Master	Ji 己 Earth	Month	Chen 辰 (Dragon)

Summary

- Bing Fire, Gui Water and Jia Wood are preferred as Useful Gods

- Where Bing Fire – the Resource Star – is present while with the absence of Gui Water, this Day Master may still be able to prosper and become wealthy in life.

- Where Gui Water – the Wealth Star – is present while with the absence of Jia Wood and Bing Fire, this Day Master may only lead an average – albeit comfortable – life.

- Where Bing Fire and Gui Water are both present, although Jia Wood may be absent, this Ji Earth Day Master would still be able to command the requisite skills and knowledge needed to succeed in life.

- Where the Earthly Branches form a complete Wood (Seven Killings) Structure, it is necessary to have Geng Metal – the Hurting Officer Star to penetrate through the Heavenly Stems and keep Wood under control, in order to maintain the balance in this Ji Earth Day Master's BaZi Chart.

Ji 己 Earth Day Master, Born in Fourth Month 四月

Si 巳 (Snake) Month
May 6th - June 5th

Do note that the dates provided above are subject to slight yearly variations. Please refer to the Ten Thousand Year Calendar for the accurate transition dates for each year.

| Day Master | Ji 己 Earth | Month | Si 巳 (Snake) |

Snake

日元 **Day Master**	月 **Month**
己 *Ji* **Yin Earth**	巳 *Si* **Snake Yin Fire**

For a Ji Earth Day Master born in a Si (Snake) Month, a Direct Resource Structure is formed where Bing Fire is revealed as one of the Heavenly Stems.

Where Geng Metal is revealed as one of the Heavenly Stems, a Hurting Officer Structure is formed.

Where Wu Earth is revealed as one of the Heavenly Stems, a Goat Blade Structure is formed when the conditions are met.

Should, however, neither Bing Fire, Geng Metal nor Wu Earth happen to be revealed within the Heavenly Stems, one should select a Structure according to the BaZi Chart's most prominent Qi attribute at one's discretion.

| Day Master | Ji 己 Earth | | Month | Si 巳 (Snake) |

喜用神提要 Regulating Useful God Reference Guide

月 Month	用神 Useful God
4th Month 四月 Si 巳 (Snake) Month	癸 *Gui* **Yin Water**　　丙 *Bing* **Yang Fire**

Snake

For a Si (Snake) Month, Gui Water and Bing Fire are the Regulating Useful Gods.

Without Gui Water, it would be impossible to 'regulate' and 'adjust' the overall Qi of this Ji Earth Day Master's BaZi Chart. And even in the presence of Gui Water, 'wet' or 'moistened' Earth simply cannot do without Bing Fire, to nourish the Earth.

| Day Master | Ji 己 Earth | Month | Si 巳 (Snake) |

6th day of May – 5th day of June, Gregorian Calendar

Fire Qi is obviously strong in a summer month. Since both Fire and Earth are strong in a Si (Snake) Month, Metal and Water will consequently tend to be 'parched' or 'dry'.

As such, Water would first be needed to 'moisten' this Ji Earth Day Master. Here, the Geng Metal Hidden Stem found inside the Si (Snake) Earthly Branch may also be employed as a Useful God, in order to produce and ensure the continuity of Water. Should this be achieveable by the conditions of the chart, a well balanced, blissful and peaceful life is expected.

Where Water is present but Metal absent, this Ji Earth Day Master may be lacking, in terms of balance and strength. Under such circumstances, this Day Master may still prosper and become wealthy in life; although his or her wealth may not be sustainable for too long.

It is undesirable for this chart to further meet Fire Qi as it weakens Metal, which is needed to produce Water as this Day Master's Useful God.

Where Metal and Water Qi happens to be strong due to the setup of the chart, Bing Fire would then be the useful god. If Metal and Water are prominent, this Day Master shall enjoy a life of nobility, power and great fortune.

四月 Fourth Month

Snake

| Day Master | Ji 己 Earth | | Month | Si 巳 (Snake) |

Commentary

In addition to the preceding narratives on the potential Structures and scenarios resulting from a Ji Earth Day Master born in a Si (Snake) Month, the following circumstances also play their respective roles in determining the overall strength of this Day Master's BaZi Chart.

Note:

- Gui Water is the preferred Useful God for this Ji Earth Day Master.

- Where the Earthly Branches form a Fire Structure – and while Water is totally missing from chart – this Ji Earth Day Master may be afflicted by loneliness and unhappiness in life.

- It would be best for this Ji Earth Day Master, where both Xin Metal and Gui Water are both present.

- It is undesirable to meet further Fire and Earth Qi.

- Where the Si (Snake), Wu (Horse) or Wei (Goat) forms the Southern Fire – this chart needs the Geng Metal and or Xin Metal to produce and ensure the continuity of Water, even if Water is already present in his or her BaZi Chart.

Snake

129

| Day Master | Ji 己 Earth | | Month | Si 巳 (Snake) |

Additional Attributes

格局 Structural Star	偏財 Indirect Wealth	正印 Direct Resource
用神 Useful God	Gui 癸 Water	Bing 丙 Fire
Conditions	Where Bing Fire and Gui Water are both revealed, this Ji Earth Day Master shall enjoy success in his or her career-related pursuits. This Ji Earth would enjoy even more success, should Xin Metal also happen to be present in his or her BaZi Chart.	
Positive Circumstances	Absense of Wu Earth in the Heavenly Stems.	
Negative Circumstances	Wu Earth that penetrates through the Heavenly Stems will counter, 'hurt' and hence weaken Gui Water, as well as Bing Fire.	

格局 Structural Star	正印 Direct Resource	偏印 Indirect Resource
用神 Useful God	Bing 丙 Fire	Ding 丁 Fire
Conditions	Where the Earthly Branches form Fire formation, Ren Water and Gui Water would be needed as Useful Gods.	
Positive Circumstances	Water, rooted in the Branches.	
Negative Circumstances	In the absence of Water.	

| Day Master | Ji 己 Earth | | Month | Si 巳 (Snake) |

Additional Attributes

格局 Structural Star	正官 Direct Officer	七殺 Seven Killings
用神 Useful God	Jia 甲 Wood	Yi 乙 Wood
Conditions	Where the Earthly Branches form a Wood and Fire Structure, both Geng Metal and Ren Water must be present, in order to consummate the situation.	
Positive Circumstances	Presence of Ren Water and Geng Metal.	
Negative Circumstances	Where Water is missing from the chart, this Ji Earth Day Master may be afflicted by loneliness throughout his or her entire life.	

Snake

* *Gui Water and Bing Fire are the preferred Useful Gods.*

** *Xin Metal is the secondary Useful God.*

| Day Master | Ji 己 Earth | Month | Si 巳 (Snake) |

Summary

- Gui Water – the Indirect Wealth Star - is the primary Useful God for a Ji Earth Day Master born in a summer month.

- Where the Earthly Branches form a Fire Structure, Ren Water should preferably be present as well.

- In the absence of Gui Water, Ren Water may be used in its stead. Likewise, in the absence of Xin Metal, Geng Metal may be used instead.

- Wu Earth should also be prevented from penetrating through the Heavenly Stems. Otherwise a full fledged Goat Blade formation may be formed. With the Goat Blade, a controlled Seven Killings Star is needed for completion of the structure.

Ji 己 Earth Day Master, Born in Fifth Month 五月

Wu 午 (Horse) Month
June 6th - July 6th

Do note that the dates provided above are subject to slight yearly variations. Please refer to the Ten Thousand Year Calendar for the accurate transition dates for each year.

五月
Fifth Month

Horse

| Day Master | Ji 己 Earth | | Month | Wu 午 (Horse) |

日元 Day Master	月 Month
己 *Ji* **Yin Earth**	午 *Wu* **Horse** **Yang Fire**

For a Ji Earth Day Master born in a Wu (Horse) Month, the Earthly Branch of Wu (Horse) is Ji Earth's 'Prosperous' position. The Thriving Structure is formed.

Where the Ding Fire appears in the Heavenly Stem, an Indirect Resource Structure may be formed depending on circumstances and chart condition.

Day Master Ji 己 Earth   **Month** Wu 午 (Horse)

喜用神提要 **Regulating Useful God Reference Guide**

月 Month	用神 Useful God
5th Month 五月 **Wu 午 (Horse) Month**	癸 *Gui* **Yin Water** 丙 *Bing* **Yang Fire**

Horse

For a Wu (Horse) Month, Gui Water is the Regulating Useful God.

Without Gui Water, it would be impossible to 'arbitrate' and 'adjust' the overall Qi of this Ji Earth Day Master's BaZi Chart.

五
月

Fifth Month

Day Master Ji 己 Earth	Month Wu 午 (Horse)

6th day of June – 6th day of July, Gregorian Calendar

The 'dry' Earth needs Water. The absence of Metal and Water would result in this Day Master becoming 'parched' or even 'burnt'. Metal and Water are both weak in this month.

As such, both Metal and Water Qi would have to be rooted so that their continuity and relevance as Useful Gods to this Ji Earth Day Master may be ensured.

Horse

It is undesirable for this Day Master to meet additional Wood and Fire Qi.

Where rooted Metal and Water is found, this chart would enjoy nobility, fame and success throughout life.

Jia Wood – the Direct Officer Star – will easily combine with the Day Master and transform into Earth. As such, Metal would be needed as a Useful God in keeping Jia Wood under control. Where Water is available to produce and 'protect' Wood, however, this Day Master shall become famous and wealthy in life.

| Day Master | Ji 己 Earth | | Month | Wu 午 (Horse) |

Commentary

In addition to the preceding narratives on the potential Structures and scenarios resulting from a Ji Earth Day Master born in a Wu (Horse) Month, the following circumstances also play their respective roles in determining the overall strength of this Day Master's BaZi Chart.

Note:

- Gui Water is the preferred Useful God for this Ji Earth Day Master.

- Where the Earthly Branches form a Fire Structure – while Water is missing from the chart – this Ji Earth Day Master may be afflicted by loneliness and misery in life.

- It would be best where both Xin Metal and Gui Water are both present and simultaneously in the chart.

- It is best to avoid meeting additional Fire and Earth, especially since Fire is already strong in summer, and has the potential to scorch the Earth.

- Geng Metal and Xin Metal are needed to produce and ensure the continuity of Water, even if Water is already present in his or her BaZi Chart.

五
月

Fifth Month

Horse

| Day Master | Ji 己 Earth | | Month | Wu 午 (Horse) |

Additional Attributes

五月
Fifth Month

Horse

格局 Structural Star	偏財 Indirect Wealth	正印 Direct Resource
用神 Useful God	Gui 癸 Water	Bing 丙 Fire
Conditions	Where Gui Water is revealed, this Ji Earth Day Master shall enjoy success in his or her career-related pursuits. This Ji Earth Day Master will enjoy even more success, should Xin Metal also happen to be present in his or her BaZi Chart.	
Positive Circumstances	Presence of Gui Water, rooted in the Earthly Branches and penetrating to the Heavenly Stems.	
Negative Circumstances	Wu Earth that penetrates through the Heavenly Stems will counter, 'hurt' and weaken Gui Water.	

格局 Structural Star	正印 Direct Resource	偏印 Indirect Resource
用神 Useful God	Bing 丙 Fire	Ding 丁 Fire
Conditions	Where the Earthly Branches form a full Fire Structure, Ren Water and Gui Water would be needed as Useful Gods.	
Positive Circumstances	Water, rooted in the Earthly Branches.	
Negative Circumstances	In the absence of Water, this Ji Earth Day Master may be afflicted by poverty and loneliness, failure and misery in life.	

| Day Master | Ji 己 Earth | | Month | Wu 午 (Horse) |

Additional Attributes

格局 Structural Star	正官 Direct Officer	七殺 Seven Killings
用神 Useful God	Jia 甲 Wood	Yi 乙 Wood
Conditions	The Earthly Branches form a Wood Structure, both Geng Metal and Ren Water must also be present, in order to consummate the situation.	
Positive Circumstances	Ren Water present in the chart.	
Negative Circumstances	Where Water is missing from the Four Pillars of Destiny, this Ji Earth Day Master may be afflicted by loneliness and hardship throughout his or her entire life.	

Horse

* Gui Water is the preferred Useful God for a Ji Earth Day Master born in a Wu (Horse) month.

** Xin Metal is the secondary Useful God.

Day Master	Ji 己 Earth	Month	Wu 午 (Horse)

Summary

- Gui Water – the Indirect Wealth Star - is the primary Useful God for a Ji Earth Day Master born in a summer month.

- Where the Earthly Branches form a Fire Structure, Ren Water should preferably be present as well.

- In the absence of Gui Water, Ren Water may be used in its stead. Likewise, in the absence of Xin Metal, Geng Metal may be used in its stead.

- The principles governing the determination of the Useful Gods for a Ji Earth Day Master born in a summer month – such as a Si (Snake), Wu (Horse) or Wei (Goat) Month – are rather similar, regardless of the specific month in question. Nevertheless, much will depend on the presence – or absence – of Ren Water and Gui Water, as the primary Useful Gods.

Ji 己 Earth Day Master, Born in Sixth Month 六月

Wei 未 (Goat) Month
July 7th - August 7th

Do note that the dates provided above are subject to slight yearly variations. Please refer to the Ten Thousand Year Calendar for the accurate transition dates for each year.

| Day Master | Ji 己 Earth | Month | Wei 未 (Goat) |

日元 **Day Master**	月 **Month**
己 *Ji* Yin Earth	未 *Wei* Goat Yin Earth

For a Ji Earth Day Master born in a Wei (Goat) Month, a Seven Killings Structure is formed where Yi Wood is revealed as one of the Heavenly Stems.

Where Ding Fire is revealed as one of the Heavenly Stems, an Indirect Resource Structure is formed.

Where the Ji Earth is also revealed as one of the Heavenly Stems, a Thriving Structure may be formed depending on the condition of the chart.

Should, however, neither Yi Wood, Ding Fire nor Ji Earth happen to be revealed within the Heavenly Stems, one should select the BaZi Chart's most prominent Qi attribute at one's discretion.

Day Master Ji 己 Earth   **Month** Wei 未 (Goat)

喜用神提要 Regulating Useful God Reference Guide

月 Month	用神 Useful God	
6th Month 六月 **Wei 未 (Goat) Month**	癸 *Gui* **Yin Water**	丙 *Bing* **Yang Fire**

Goat

For a Wei (Goat) Month, Gui Water and Bing Fire are the Regulating Useful Gods.

Without Gui Water, it would be impossible to 'arbitrate' and 'adjust' the overall hot Qi of this chart.

| Day Master | Ji 己 Earth | Month | Wei 未 (Goat) |

7th day of July – 7th day of August, Gregorian Calendar

This is a month where Earth is dominant and extremely strong.

Earth is also very 'dry' in a Wei (Goat) Month, and Water is needed as a Useful God to 'moisten' Earth.

Where Wood is also available to 'loosen' Earth, this Ji Earth Day Master shall become powerful and authoritative in life.

Goat

Metal and Water are the primary Useful Gods for a Ji Earth Day Master born in a chart where Fire and Earth are strong. This is in order to prevent Wood from becoming overly strong or abundance, as well as Water from being weakened.

Metal and Water, under such circumstances, can hence be used to support and strengthen this Ji Earth Day Master.

It is undesirable for this chart to further meet Fire Qi.

Day Master	Ji 己 Earth	Month	Wei 未 (Goat)

Commentary

In addition to the preceding narratives on the potential Structures and scenarios resulting from a Ji Earth Day Master born in a Wei (Goat) Month, the following circumstances also play their respective roles in determining the overall strength of this Day Master's BaZi Chart.

Goat

Note:

- Gui Water is the most-preferred Useful God for this Ji Earth Day Master.

- Where the Earthly Branches form a Fire Structure – a possible Follow The Prosperous structure may be formed. Where such a structure is successfully formed, an extraordinary life is expected. One that brings great wealth, power and fame.

- In ordinary circumstances, it would be best for this Ji Earth Day Master to have both Xin Metal and Gui Water both present in the chart.

- It is best to avoid meeting additional Fire and Earth, especially since Fire is already strong in summer, and has the potential to 'dry' and crack the Earth.

- Where Wood and Fire are present in abundance – while Water is missing from the BaZi Chart and while no special structure is formed, this person may be afflicted by loneliness, hardship and misery in life.

- Geng Metal and Xin Metal are needed to produce and ensure the continuity of Water, even if Water is already present in his or her BaZi Chart.

145

Day Master	Ji 己 Earth	Month	Wei 未 (Goat)

Additional Attributes

格局 Structural Star	偏財 Indirect Wealth	正印 Direct Resource
用神 Useful God	Gui 癸 Water	Bing 丙 Fire
Conditions	Where Gui Water is revealed, this Ji Earth Day Master shall enjoy success in his or her career-related pursuits. This chart will enjoy even more success, should Xin Metal also happen to be present in his or her BaZi Chart.	
Positive Circumstances	Gui Water that is rooted in the Earthly Branches and penetrating to the Heavenly Stems.	
Negative Circumstances	Wu Earth that penetrates through the Heavenly Stems will combine away the Gui Water.	

格局 Structural Star	正印 Direct Resource	偏印 Indirect Resource
用神 Useful God	Bing 丙 Fire	Ding 丁 Fire
Conditions	Where the Earthly Branches form a full Fire Structure, Ren Water and Gui Water would be needed as Useful Gods.	
Positive Circumstances	Water rooted in the Earthly branches.	
Negative Circumstances	In the absence of Water, this Ji Earth Day Master may be afflicted by poverty and loneliness in life.	

| Day Master | Ji 己 Earth | | Month | Wei 未 (Goat) |

Additional Attributes

格局 Structural Star	正官 Direct Officer	七殺 Seven Killings
用神 Useful God	Jia 甲 Wood	Yi 乙 Wood
Conditions	Where Earthly Branches form a full Wood Formation, both Geng Metal and Ren Water must also be present, in order to consummate the situation.	
Positive Circumstances	Ren Water present. Gui may be a substitute should Ren is absent.	
Negative Circumstances	Where Water is missing from chart, this Ji Earth Day Master may be afflicted by loneliness throughout his or her entire life.	

Goat

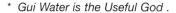

* *Gui Water is the Useful God .*

** *Xin Metal is the secondary Useful God*

六月 Sixth Month

| Day Master | Ji 己 Earth | Month | Wei 未 (Goat) |

Goat

Summary

- Gui Water – the Indirect Wealth Star - is the primary Useful God for a Ji Earth Day Master born in this summer month.

- Where the Earthly Branches form a full Fire Structure, Ren Water should preferably be present as well, in order to arrive at a best-case scenario for this Day Master.

- Where Ren Water is absent and Fire and Earth Qi are in abundance, this chart may form a Follow The Prosperous structure. Where the Structure is successfully formed, this chart belongs to the extraordinary achiever. A life of greatness awaits.

- In the absence of Gui Water, Ren Water may be used in its stead. Likewise, in the absence of Xin Metal, Geng Metal may be used in its stead.

- The principles governing the determination of the Useful Gods for a Ji Earth Day Master born in a summer month – such as a Si (Snake), Wu (Horse) or Wei (Goat) Month – are rather similar, regardless of the specific month in question.

Ji 己 Earth Day Master, Born in Seventh Month 七月

Shen 申 (Monkey) Month
August 8th - September 7th

Do note that the dates provided above are subject to slight yearly variations. Please refer to the Ten Thousand Year Calendar for the accurate transition dates for each year.

七月 Seventh Month

Monkey

Day Master Ji 己 Earth	Month Shen 申 (Monkey)

日元 Day Master	月 Month
己 *Ji* **Yin Earth**	申 *Shen* **Monkey** **Yang Metal**

For a Ji Earth Day Master born in a Shen (Monkey) Month, a Hurting Officer Structure is formed where Geng Metal is revealed as one of the Heavenly Stems.

Where Ren Water is revealed as one of the Heavenly Stems, a Direct Wealth Structure is formed.

Where the Wu Earth is revealed as one of the Heavenly Stems, a Goat Blade Structure may be formed when the conditions of the chart supports this.

Should, however, neither Geng Metal, Ren Water nor Wu Earth happen to be revealed amongst the Heavenly Stems, one should select a Structure according to the BaZi Chart's most prominent Qi attribute at one's discretion.

Day Master	Ji 己 Earth		Month	Shen 申 (Monkey)

喜用神提要 Regulating Useful God Reference Guide

月 Month	用神 Useful God
7th Month 七月 Shen 申 (Monkey) Month	丙 *Bing* **Yang Fire** 癸 *Gui* **Yin Water**

七月 Seventh Month

Monkey

For a Shen (Monkey) Month, Bing Fire and Gui Water are the Regulating Useful Gods.

Bing Fire provides 'warmth' for this Ji Earth Day Master, while Gui Water serves to 'moisten' it.

Geng Metal is strong in a Shen (Monkey) Month and as such, Bing Fire may be used to keep Metal Qi under control. In a similar vein, Gui Water may also be used to weaken and keep Metal Qi under control.

| Day Master | Ji 己 Earth | | Month | Shen 申 (Monkey) |

8th day of August – 7th day of September, Gregorian Calendar

Metal Qi is dominant while Water is strong this month. Due to their individual and combined strength, Metal and Water have the capacity to weaken Fire, and 'thin' the Earth.

Since the Shen (Monkey) Month denotes early autumn, the Qi surrounding this Ji Earth Day Master is becoming gradually colder. This is why Fire is needed to provide 'warmth' for this Day Master, which should also be aided and supported by more 'hot' or 'warm' Earth. Then and only then will this Day Master be 'solid' and strong.

Care should be taken, whenever Wood is used. Although Jia Wood does combine with this Ji Earth Day Master to produce Earth, Earth would still be weak. Under such circumstances, Fire would be needed to keep Metal Qi under control, and to provide 'warmth' for this Day Master.

| Day Master | Ji 己 Earth | Month | Shen 申 (Monkey) |

Commentary

In addition to the preceding narratives on the potential Structures and scenarios resulting from a Ji Earth Day Master born in a Shen (Monkey) Month, the following circumstances also play their respective roles in determining the overall strength of this Day Master's BaZi Chart.

Note:

Monkey

- Bing Fire is the primary or preferred Useful God

- Gui Water as the secondary Useful God.

- Where a Metal Structure is formed, Fire must also be present and seen in the chart. Without Fire, the person is very talented, but find his talent contributing to his major problems in life.

Day Master	Ji 己 Earth	Month	Shen 申 (Monkey)

Additional Attributes

格局 **Structural Star**	偏財 Indirect Wealth	正印 Direct Resource
用神 **Useful God**	Gui 癸 Water	Bing 丙 Fire
Conditions	Should both Bing Fire and Gui Water Useful Gods be present, this Ji Earth Day Master shall be blessed with fame and fortune in life.	
Positive Circumstances	Bing Fire in the Heavenly Stems and Gui Water rooted in the Earthl Branches.	
Negative Circumstances	Wu Earth penetrates through the Heavenly Stems.	

格局 **Structural Star**	正財 Direct Wealth
用神 **Useful God**	Ren 壬 Water
Conditions	Even if Ren Water were to be revealed in the Heavenly Stems, it would not be as good or beneficial compared to if Gui Water being revealed. Ji Earth finds it hard to control Ren Water. Bing Fire should not be absent from this chart.
Positive Circumstances	Bing Fire – the Direct Resource Star – penetrates through the Heavenly Stems.
Negative Circumstances	In the absence of Bing Fire this person shall still be knowledgeable and learned; although any material success he or she enjoys in life may be limited.

Day Master	Ji 己 Earth	Month	Shen 申 (Monkey)

Additional Attributes

格局 Structural Star	傷官 Hurting Officer	食神 Eating God
用神 Useful God	Geng 庚 Metal	Xin 辛 Metal
Conditions	Where the Earthly Branches forms a full Metal Structure, and Gui Water – the Indirect Wealth Star – is revealed in the Heavenly Stems, this Ji Earth Day Master shall enjoy prosperity in life.	
Positive Circumstances	Bing Fire and Ding Fire must not only be present, but also seen penetrating through the Heavenly Stems.	
Negative Circumstances	Neither Bing Fire nor Ding Fire is present in this Ji Earth Day Master's BaZi Chart.	

Monke

格局 Structural Star	劫財 Rob Wealth	比肩 Friend
用神 Useful God	Wu 戊 Earth	Ji 己 Earth
Conditions	The entire chart is made up of Earth and Metal Qi. Special Follow the Son Structure may be formed.	
Positive Circumstances	Absense of Wood Qi.	
Negative Circumstances	Presence of Wood Qi.	

| Day Master | Ji 己 Earth | Month | Shen 申 (Monkey) |

Additional Attributes

格局 Structural Star	正印 Direct Resource	偏印 Indirect Resource
用神 Useful God	Bing 丙 Fire	Ding 丁 Fire
Conditions	It would be highly unfavourable to this Ji Earth Day Master, where the Earthly Branches form a full Fire Structure, with Water also missing from the Four Pillars of Destiny.	
Positive Circumstances	Presence of Water in the chart.	
Negative Circumstances	Wu Earth is revealed, and weakens Ren Water and Gui Water.	

* Bing Fire and Gui Water are the preferred Useful Gods

| Day Master | Ji 己 Earth | Month | Shen 申 (Monkey) |

Summary

- Where the special formation of Follow The Son is formed, this person shall enjoy recognition, fame and great wealth.
- Fire Qi is essential for the vitality of this Earth.

Monke

七
月

Seventh Month

157

Ji 己 Earth Day Master,
Born in Eighth Month 八月

You 酉 (Rooster) Month
September 8th - October 7th

Do note that the dates provided above are subject to slight yearly variations. Please refer to the Ten Thousand Year Calendar for the accurate transition dates for each year.

BaZi Structures & Structural Useful Gods 格局與格局用神

Day Master	Ji 己 Earth

Month	You 酉 (Rooster)

日元 Day Master	月 Month
己 Ji Yin Earth	酉 You Rooster Yin Metal

For a Ji Earth Day Master born in a You (Rooster) Month, an Eating God Structure is formed where Xin Metal is revealed or not revealed as one of the Heavenly Stems in the chart.

Day Master	Ji 己 Earth		Month	You 酉 (Rooster)

喜用神提要 Regulating Useful God Reference Guide

月 Month	用神 Useful God	
8th Month 八月 **You** 酉 **(Rooster) Month**	丙 *Bing* **Yang Fire**	癸 *Gui* **Yin Water**

酉 Rooster

Bing Fire and Gui Water are the Regulating Useful Gods.

| Day Master | Ji 己 Earth | | Month | You 酉 (Rooster) |

8th day of September - 7th day of October, Gregorian Calendar

Metal is at its strongest this month.

Such strong Metal Qi would invariably weaken the Qi of this Ji Earth Day Master. Without Fire and Earth to produce and strengthen this Day Master, the chart would be a lackluster.

It is unnecessary for this chart to meet additional Water, since Metal, being already strong, would produce an abundance of Water.

There is no need to further meet additional Wood Qi, which would invariably weaken the Ji Earth further.

In a You (Rooster) Month, a Ji Earth Day Master born in an hour when Fire and Earth is strong, would be possessed of a genteel, refined and cultured disposition.

| Day Master | Ji 己 Earth | Month | You 酉 (Rooster) |

Commentary

In addition to the preceding narratives on the potential Structures and scenarios resulting from a Ji Earth Day Master born in a You (Rooster) Month, the following circumstances also play their respective roles in determining the overall strength of this Day Master's BaZi Chart.

Note :

- Bing Fire is the primary Useful God for a Ji Earth Day Master born in a Shen (Monkey), You (Rooster) or Xu (Dog) Month, with Gui Water as the secondary Useful God.

- Where a Fire Qi is revealed in the Heavenly Stems or Earthly Branches, Water must also be present and seen.

- Where a full Metal Structure is formed, Fire must be present and seen. Otherwise, this Ji Earth Day Master may be afflicted by loneliness and hatred in life.

- Since the Qi and the overall environment is becoming gradually colder, given that the Shen (Monkey), You (Rooster) and Xu (Dog) Months denote autumn, Fire is certainly one of the most preferred Useful Gods.

八月

Eighth Month

Rooster

Day Master	Ji 己 Earth	Month	You 酉 (Rooster)

Additional Attributes

格局 Structural Star	偏財 Indirect Wealth	正印 Direct Resource
用神 Useful God	Gui 癸 Water	Bing 丙 Fire
Conditions	Gui Water should be employed as the primary Useful God, with Bing Fire –as the secondary Useful God. Should both Useful Gods be present, this Ji Earth Day Master shall be blessed with fame, happiness and good fortune in life.	
Positive Circumstances	Gui Water and Bing Fire present in the chart.	
Negative Circumstances	Wu Earth penetrates through the Heavenly Stems.	

格局 Structural Star	正財 Direct Wealth
用神 Useful God	Ren 壬 Water
Conditions	Ji Earth does not handle Ren Water very well.
Positive Circumstances	Bing Fire penetrates through the Heavenly Stems.
Negative Circumstances	In the absence of Bing Fire this person would still be knowledgeable and learned; but any material success he or she enjoys in life may be severely limited.

Day Master	Ji 己 Earth		Month	You 酉 (Rooster)

Additional Attributes

格局 Structural Star	傷官 Hurting Officer	食神 Eating God
用神 Useful God	Geng 庚 Metal	Xin 辛 Metal
Conditions	Where the Earthly Branches forms a complete Metal Structure, and Gui Water –is revealed in the Heavenly Stems, this Ji Earth Day Master shall enjoy fame through his knowledge, skill or talent.	
Positive Circumstances	Bing Fire and Ding Fire must not only be present, but also seen penetrating through the Heavenly Stems.	
Negative Circumstances	Neither Bing Fire nor Ding Fire is present in this Ji Earth Day Master's BaZi Chart.	

Rooste

格局 Structural Star	劫財 Rob Wealth	比肩 Friend
用神 Useful God	Wu 戊 Earth	Ji 己 Earth
Conditions	Where both Rob Wealth and Friend Stars are in abundance in this chart, Wood is needed to loosen the Earth.	
Positive Circumstances	Presence of Wood Qi.	
Negative Circumstances	Without Jia Wood revealed in the Heavenly Stems, this Ji Earth Day Master may be afflicted by loneliness in life.	

| Day Master | Ji 己 Earth | Month | You 酉 (Rooster) |

Additional Attributes

格局 **Structural Star**	正印 Direct Resource	偏印 Indirect Resource
用神 **Useful God**	Bing 丙 Fire	Ding 丁 Fire
Conditions	It would be highly unfavourable to this Ji Earth Day Master, where the Earthly Branches form a Fire Structure, with Water also missing from the Four Pillars of Destiny.	
Positive Circumstances	Presence of water at least in the Earthly Branches.	
Negative Circumstances	Wu Earth is revealed, and 'hurts' the Ren Water and Gui Water.	

* *Bing Fire and Gui Water are the preferred Useful Gods*

八月 Eighth Month

酉 Rooster

166

| Day Master | Ji 己 Earth | Month | You 酉 (Rooster) |

Summary

- Where the Four Graveyard Earthly Branches of Chen (Dragon), Xu (Dog), Chou (Ox) and Wei (Goat) are present – without Jia Wood to penetrate through the Heavenly Stems – this Ji Earth Day Master may be afflicted by loneliness and poverty in life.

- Fire is needed to control the excessive Metal and sustain the vitality of the Earth.

Rooster

Ji 己 Earth Day Master, Born in Ninth Month 九月

Xu 戌 (Dog) Month
October 8th - November 6th

Do note that the dates provided above are subject to slight yearly variations. Please refer to the Ten Thousand Year Calendar for the accurate transition dates for each year.

BaZi Structures & Structural Useful Gods 格局與格局用神

| Day Master Ji 己 Earth | Month Xu 戌 (Dog) |

日元 Day Master	月 Month
己 *Ji* **Yin Earth**	戌 *Xu* **Dog** **Yang Earth**

For a Ji Earth Day Master born in a Xu (Dog) Month, an Indirect Resource Structure is formed where Ding Fire is revealed as one of the Heavenly Stems.

Where Xin Metal is revealed as one of the Heavenly Stems, an Eating God Structure is formed.

Where the Wu Earth is revaled as one of the Heavenly Stems, a Thriving Structure may be formed depending on the surrounding circumstances.

Should, however, neither Ding Fire nor Xin Metal happen to be revealed amongst the Heavenly Stems, one should select a Structure according to the BaZi Chart's most prominent Qi attribute at one's discretion.

| Day Master | Ji 己 Earth | | Month | Xu 戌 (Dog) |

喜用神提要 Regulating Useful God Reference Guide

月 Month	用神 Useful God
9th Month 九月 **Xu** 戌 **(Dog) Month**	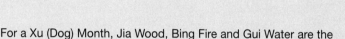 甲 *Jia* **Yang Wood**　　丙 *Bing* **Yang Fire**　　癸 *Gui* **Yin Water**

戌 Dog

For a Xu (Dog) Month, Jia Wood, Bing Fire and Gui Water are the Regulating Useful Gods.

Earth Qi is prominent in a Xu (Dog) Month. This is where Jia Wood may be employed as a Useful God, to 'loosen' Earth.

Meanwhile, Bing Fire and Gui Water serve as secondary Useful Gods to this Ji Earth Day Master.

Day Master	Ji 己 Earth	**Month**	Xu 戌 (Dog)

8th day of October – 6th day of November, Gregorian Calendar

The Xu (Dog) Earthly Branch serves as 'storage' for excess Fire and Earth Qi.

This Day Master is in danger of becoming overly 'dry' or 'parched'. As such, Water is a necessary Useful God, in providing much-needed 'moisture'.

It would also be preferable to have Metal to produce Water to 'moisten' Earth; instead of using Wood alone. This is because where Earth is 'leaden' and 'thick', Wood would tend to be more brittle, and hence too weak to be of effective use alone.

A Ji Earth Day Master born in an hour when Metal and Water happen to be strong may even be born into the lap of luxury, and enjoy a life of affluence and wealth.

戌

Dog

Day Master	Ji 己 Earth	Month	Xu 戌 (Dog)

Commentary

In addition to the preceding narratives on the potential Structures and scenarios resulting from a Ji Earth Day Master born in a Xu (Dog) Month, the following circumstances also play their respective roles in determining the overall strength of this Day Master's BaZi Chart.

Note:

Dog

- Gui Water is the primary or preferred Useful God for a Ji Earth Day Master born in Xu (Dog) Month, with Bing and Jia Wood as the secondary Useful God.

- Even though Earth is strong in a Xu (Dog) Month, Jia Wood is still needed to penetrate through the Heavenly Stems, in order to loosen the Earth.

- Where a full Fire Structure is formed, Water must also be present and seen.

- Where a full Metal formation is formed, Fire must also be present and seen. Otherwise, this Ji Earth Day Master may be afflicted by hardship, unhappiness and burdens in life.

| Day Master | Ji 己 Earth | | Month | Xu 戌 (Dog) |

Additional Attributes

戊 Dog

格局 Structural Star	偏財 Indirect Wealth	正印 Direct Resource
用神 Useful God	Gui 癸 Water	Bing 丙 Fire
Conditions	Gui Water should be employed as the primary Useful God, with Bing Fire –as the secondary Useful God. Should both Useful Gods be present, this Ji Earth Day Master shall be blessed with fame and fortune in life.	
Positive Circumstances	Presence of Bing Fire and Gui Water.	
Negative Circumstances	Wu Earth penetrates through the Heavenly Stems.	

格局 Structural Star	正財 Direct Wealth
用神 Useful God	Ren 壬 Water
Conditions	Gui is more effective for Ji Earth than Ren Water. However, with Fire Qi, Ji Earth is able to use Ren Water. Bing Fire should not be absent from this Day Master's BaZi Chart.
Positive Circumstances	Bing Fire penetrating through the Heavenly Stems.
Negative Circumstances	In the absence of Bing Fire this Ji Earth Day Master shall still be knowledgeable and learned; but any material success he or she enjoys in life may be shortlived.

| Day Master | Ji 己 Earth | | Month | Xu 戌 (Dog) |

Additional Attributes

格局 Structural Star	傷官 Hurting Officer	食神 Eating God
用神 Useful God	Geng 庚 Metal	Xin 辛 Metal
Conditions	Where the Earthly Branches forms a full a Metal Structure, and Gui Water –is revealed in the Heavenly Stems, this Ji Earth Day Master shall long lasting fame and recognition.	
Positive Circumstances	Bing Fire and Ding Fire must not only be present, but also seen penetrating through the Heavenly Stems.	
Negative Circumstances	Neither Bing Fire nor Ding Fire is present in this Ji Earth Day Master's BaZi Chart.	

Dog

格局 Structural Star	劫財 Rob Wealth	比肩 Friend
用神 Useful God	Wu 戊 Earth	Ji 己 Earth
Conditions	Where the Four Graveyard Earthly Branches of Chen (Dragon), Xu (Dog), Chou (Ox) and Wei (Goat) are all present – while Jia Wood is also revealed in the Heavenly Stems – this Ji Earth Day Master shall prosper and become wealthy in life.	
Positive Circumstances	Presence of Jia Wood revealing in the Heavenly Stems.	
Negative Circumstances	Without Jia Wood revealed in the Heavenly Stems, this Ji Earth Day Master may be afflicted by suffering, hardship and pain in life.	

Day Master Ji 己 Earth	**Month** Xu 戌 (Dog)

Additional Attributes

格局 **Structural Star**	正印 Direct Resource	偏印 Indirect Resource
用神 **Useful God**	Bing 丙 Fire	Ding 丁 Fire
Conditions	It would be highly unfavourable to this Ji Earth Day Master, where the Earthly Branches form a full Fire Structure, when Water also missing from the chart.	
Positive Circumstances	Presence of Water Qi.	
Negative Circumstances	Wu Earth is revealed, and 'hurts' the Ren Water and Gui Water.	

* Bing Fire and Gui Water are the preferred Useful Gods for a Ji Earth Day Master born in a Xu (Dog) Month.

Day Master	Ji 己 Earth		Month	Xu 戌 (Dog)

Summary

- Where the Four Graveyard Earthly Branches of Chen (Dragon), Xu (Dog), Chou (Ox) and Wei (Goat) are present – without Jia Wood to penetrate through the Heavenly Stems – this Ji Earth Day Master may be afflicted by loneliness, hardship, sadness and poverty in life.

- Fire is needed to keep the vitality of the Earth.

戌
Dog

177

Ji 己 Earth Day Master, Born in Tenth Month 十月

Hai 亥 (Pig) Month
November 7th - December 6th

Do note that the dates provided above are subject to slight yearly variations. Please refer to the Ten Thousand Year Calendar for the accurate transition dates for each year.

| Day Master | Ji 己 Earth | Month | Hai 亥 (Pig) |

日元 **Day Master**	月 **Month**
己 *Ji* **Yin Earth**	亥 *Hai* **Pig** **Yin Water**

For a Ji Earth Day Master born in a Pig (Hai) Month, a Direct Wealth Structure is formed where Ren Water is revealed as one of the Heavenly Stems.

Where Jia Wood is revealed as one of the Heavenly Stems, a Direct Officer Structure is formed.

Should, however, neither Ren Water nor Jia Wood happen to be revealed amongst the Heavenly Stems, one should select a Structure according to the BaZi Chart's most prominent Qi attribute at one's discretion.

Day Master	Ji 己 Earth	Month	Hai 亥 (Pig)

喜用神提要 Regulating Useful God Reference Guide

月 Month	用神 Useful God
10th Month 十月 Hai 亥 (Pig) Month	丙 甲 戊 *Bing* *Jia* *Wu* **Yang Fire** **Yang Wood** **Yang Earth**

Pig

Bing Fire, Jia Wood and Wu Earth are the Regulating Useful Gods.

A Ji Earth Day Master born in any of the winter months of Hai (Pig), Zi (Rat) and Chou (Ox) would definitely need Bing Fire to provide 'warmth'. Otherwise, it would be difficult for this Day Master to survive the cold.

Ren Water is very strong in early winter. This is why Wu Earth is needed to keep Ren Water under control.

Where Earth is present in abundance, Jia Wood may be used to 'loosen' it.

BaZi Structures & Structural Useful Gods 格局與格局用神

十月 Tenth Month

亥 Pig

Day Master	Ji 己 Earth	Month	Hai 亥 (Pig)

7th day of November – 6th day of December, Gregorian Calendar

The Chart's Qi would invariably tend to be cold, with Earth weak. Even though Water is strong and able to 'moisten' Wood, it would still be difficult for the latter to be produced. In fact, Wood is frozen in this period.

'Warm' Earth and Fire would be of use here, in supporting and strengthening this Ji Earth Day Master. It would also be preferable to avoid meeting additional Metal and Water and Wood, where possible.

This is because Metal, Water and Wood will collectively control and weaken this Ji Earth Day Master.

The wealth luck of a Ji Earth Day Master, born in an hour when Fire and Earth happen to be strong, is excellent. The fortunes of a Ji Earth Day Master born during this month will greatly depend on the availability or absence of Fire and Earth Qi in his or her BaZi Chart.

182

Day Master Ji 己 Earth	Month Hai 亥 (Pig)

Commentary

In addition to the preceding narratives on the potential Structures and scenarios resulting from a Ji Earth Day Master born in a Hai (Pig) Month, the following circumstances also play their respective roles in determining the overall strength of this Day Master's BaZi Chart.

Note:

- Bing Fire and Jia Wood are the primary Useful Gods for a Ji Earth Day Master born in a Hai (Pig), Zi (Rat) or Chou (Ox) Month.

- It is undesirable to have Ren Water and Gui penetrating through the Heavenly Stems.

- Where Ren Water is revealed in the Heavenly Stems or Earthly Branches – while Bing Fire is missing – this Ji Earth Day Master may lack a sense of purpose and direction in life.

- Where Gui Water is revealed in the Heavenly Stems or Earthly Branches – while Companion and Resource Stars are completely missing – a Follow the Wealth Structure is formed in the BaZi Chart. Under such circumstances, this Ji Earth Day Master shall enjoy an extraordinary life of adventure and success.

- Where Wu Earth and Ji Earth penetrate through the Heavenly Stems – together with Jia Wood – this Ji Earth Day Master shall possess the knowledge and skills needed to succeed in life. Nevertheless, Bing Fire must not be missing from the BaZi Chart.

- Where Geng Metal penetrates through the Heavenly Stems, Bing Fire and Ding Fire must also be strong, in order that this Ji Earth Day Master to enjoy prolonged prosperity, happiness and fame.

- Regardless of what structure this Ji Earth Day Master may enter into or encounter, Bing Fire must always be present in the chart.

十月

Tenth Month

Pig

十月

Tenth Month

亥
Pig

Day Master Ji 己 Earth		**Month** Hai 亥 (Pig)

Additional Attributes

格局 **Structural Star**	正印 Direct Resource	正官 Direct Officer
用神 **Useful God**	Bing 丙 Fire	Jia 甲 Wood
Conditions	Where Bing Fire and Jia Wood are both present, this Ji Earth Day Master shall become famous and succeed in his or her career-related pursuits.	
Positive Circumstances	Where Ren Water is present, Wu Earth would be needed to keep it under control.	
Negative Circumstances	Ren Water penetrates through the Heavenly Stems.	

格局 **Structural Star**	偏財 Indirect Wealth
用神 **Useful God**	Gui 癸 Water
Conditions	Where the Earthly Branches forms a full Water Structure – coupled with the absence of Companion and Resource Stars – a Follow the Wealth Structure may be formed.
Positive Circumstances	Absence of Companion and Resource Stars.
Negative Circumstances	Where Companion and Resource Stars penetrate through the Heavenly Stems, this Ji Earth Day Master may only lead an average life, at best.

Day Master Ji 己 Earth		**Month** Hai 亥 (Pig)

Additional Attributes

格局 **Structural Star**	劫財 Rob Wealth	比肩 Friend
用神 **Useful God**	Wu 戊 Earth	Ji 己 Earth
Conditions	Where the Four Graveyard Earthly Branches of Chen (Dragon), Xu (Dog), Chou (Ox) and Wei (Goat) are present form an Earth Structure, Jia Wood is needed to penetrate through the Heavenly Stems.	
Positive Circumstances	Jia Wood in the Heavenly Stems.	
Negative Circumstances	No Jia Wood to penetrate through the Heavenly Stems.	

Pig

格局 **Structural Star**	傷官 Hurting Officer
用神 **Useful God**	Geng 庚 Metal
Conditions	Where Ding Fire Resource Stars are seen penetrating through the Heavenly Stems, this Ji Earth Day Master shall enjoy prosperity and success throughout his/her life.
Positive Circumstances	Ding Fire rooted and strong.
Negative Circumstances	Absence of Ding Fire.

* *Bing Fire and Jia Wood are the preferred Useful Gods*

Day Master	Ji 己 Earth		Month	Hai 亥 (Pig)

Summary

- Bing Fire is needed for survival of Ji Earth born in this month.

- A Ji Earth Day Master born in a winter month should use Ding Fire to keep Geng Metal under control.

- The formation of a Follow the Wealth Structure will greatly depend on the presence and strength of this Day Master's Indirect Wealth Stars. Where the structure is successfully form, an extraordinary life of adventure and wealth awaits.

- It would be best to have both Metal – the Hurting Officer Stars – and Fire – the Resource Stars – present. This ensures long term success and happiness.

- Where Water is present in abundance, Wu Earth the Rob Wealth Star – may be used to keep it under control. In this matter, Ji Earth – a Friend Star – would be of no use.

Ji 己 Earth Day Master, Born in Eleventh Month 十一月

Zi 子 (Rat) Month
December 7th - January 5th

Do note that the dates provided above are subject to slight yearly variations. Please refer to the Ten Thousand Year Calendar for the accurate transition dates for each year.

| Day Master | Ji 己 Earth | Month | Zi 子 (Rat) |

日元 Day Master	月 Month
己 *Ji* **Yin Earth**	子 *Zi* **Rat** **Yang Water**

For a Ji Earth Day Master born in a Zi (Rat) Month, an Indirect Wealth Structure is formed where Gui Water is revealed as one of the Heavenly Stems.

Even if Gui Water is not revealed as a Heavenly Stem, an Indirect Wealth Structure would still be considered to have been formed.

| Day Master | Ji 己 Earth | Month | Zi 子 (Rat) |

喜用神提要 Regulating Useful God Reference Guide

Rat

月 Month	用神 Useful God
11th Month 十一月 **Zi 子 (Rat) Month**	丙 *Bing* **Yang Fire** 甲 *Jia* **Yang Wood** 戊 *Wu* **Yang Earth**

Bing Fire, Jia Wood and Wu Earth are the Regulating Useful Gods.

A Ji Earth Day Master born in any of the winter months of Hai (Pig), Zi (Rat) and Chou (Ox) would definitely need Bing Fire to provide 'warmth'. Otherwise, it would be difficult for this Day Master to survive the cold.

Water Qi may be in excess this month. This is why Wu Earth is needed to keep the Water Qi under control.

Where Earth is present in abundance, Jia Wood may be used to 'loosen' it.

Day Master Ji 己 Earth	**Month** Zi 子 (Rat)

7th day of December – 5th day of January, Gregorian Calendar

The Qi would invariably tend to be very cold this month.

As such, Fire would be needed to bring 'warmth' to this Day Master, while 'hot' or 'warm' Earth would be needed to keep strong Water under control. Then and only then will this Ji Earth Day Master have vitality.

It is only when Fire is seen penetrating through the Heavenly Stems that Wood may be also employed as a Useful God to this Day Master. Indeed, warm and dry Wood – i.e. Wood that harbors Fire Qi within it – will ensure the continuity of Fire Qi.

'Cold' Metal shall certainly produce 'cold' icy Water. This would only result in an extremely 'murky' or 'muddy' scenario, more so when Water comes into contact with Earth.

It is therefore undesirable for this Day Master to meet additional Metal and Water Qi.

十一月

Eleventh Month

Rat

| Day Master | Ji 己 Earth | Month | Zi 子 (Rat) |

Commentary

In addition to the preceding narratives on the potential Structures and scenarios resulting from a Ji Earth Day Master born in a Zi (Rat) Month, the following circumstances also play their respective roles in determining the overall strength of this Day Master's BaZi Chart.

Note:

- Bing Fire and Jia Wood are the primary Useful Gods for a Ji Earth Day Master born in a Hai (Pig), Zi (Rat) or Chou (Ox) Month.

- It is undesirable to have Ren Water and Gui Water penetrating through the Heavenly Stems.

- Where Ren Water is revealed in the Heavenly Stems or Earthly Branches – while Bing Fire is missing – this Ji Earth Day Master may lack a sense of purpose and direction in life.

- Where Gui Water is revealed in the Heavenly Stems or Earthly Branches – while Companion and Resource Stars are missing – a Follow the Wealth Structure may be formed in the BaZi Chart. If the formation is successful, this will be the chart of an extraordinary life.

- Where Wu Earth and Ji Earth penetrate through the Heavenly Stems – together with Jia Wood – this Ji Earth Day Master shall possess the knowledge and skills needed to succeed in life. Nevertheless, Bing Fire must not be missing from the BaZi Chart.

- Where Geng Metal penetrates through the Heavenly Stems, Bing Fire and Ding Fire must also be strong.

- Regardless of what structure this Ji Earth Day Master may enter into or encounter, Bing Fire must always be present in the chart.

Day Master Ji 己 Earth		Month Zi 子 (Rat)

Additional Attributes

格局 Structural Star	正印 Direct Resource	正官 Direct Officer
用神 Useful God	Bing 丙 Fire	Jia 甲 Wood
Conditions	Where Bing Fire and Jia Wood are both present, this Ji Earth Day Master shall enjoy recognition and fame . This person shall also enjoy success in his/her career-related pursuits.	
Positive Circumstances	Where Ren Water is present, Wu Earth would be needed to keep it under control.	
Negative Circumstances	Ren Water penetrates through the Heavenly Stems.	

格局 Structural Star	偏財 Indirect Wealth
用神 Useful God	Gui 癸 Water
Conditions	Where the Earthly Branches form a full Water Structure – coupled with the absence of Companion and Resource Stars – a Follow the Wealth Structure may be formed.
Positive Circumstances	Absense of Companion and Resource Stars.
Negative Circumstances	Where Companion and Resource Stars penetrate through the Heavenly Stems, this Ji Earth Day Master may only lead an average life, at best.

十一月 Eleventh Month

Rat

Day Master	Ji 己 Earth		Month	Zi 子 (Rat)

Rat

Additional Attributes

格局 Structural Star	劫財 Rob Wealth	比肩 Friend
用神 Useful God	Wu 戊 Earth	Ji 己 Earth
Conditions	Where the Four Graveyard Earthly Branches of Chen (Dragon), Xu (Dog), Chou (Ox) and Wei (Goat) are present form an Earth Structure, Jia Wood is needed to penetrate through the Heavenly Stems. This would ensure long term prosperity and good fortune.	
Positive Circumstances	Jia Wood in the Heavenly Stems.	
Negative Circumstances	No Jia Wood to penetrate through the Heavenly Stems.	

格局 Structural Star	傷官 Hurting Officer
用神 Useful God	Geng 庚 Metal
Conditions	Where Ding Fire is seen penetrating through the Heavenly Stems, this Ji Earth Day Master shall enjoy good fortune.
Positive Circumstances	-
Negative Circumstances	-

* Bing Fire and Jia Wood are the preferred Useful Gods for a Ji Earth Day Master born in a Hai (Pig), Zi (Rat) or Chou (Ox) Month.

193

| Day Master | Ji 己 Earth | | Month | Zi 子 (Rat) |

Summary

- Bing Fire is an essential for the survival of Ji Earth born in this month.

- A Ji Earth Day Master born in a winter month should use Ding Fire to keep Geng Metal under control.

- The formation of a Follow the Wealth Structure will greatly depend on the presence and strength of this Day Master's Indirect Wealth Stars. Where the structure is successfully form, an extraordinary life of adventure and wealth awaits.

- Where Gui Water penetrates to the Heavenly Stems, Wu Earth is needed to keep the Water at bay.

Ji 己 Earth Day Master, Born in Twelfth Month 十二月

Chou 丑 (Ox) Month
January 6th - February 3rd

Do note that the dates provided above are subject to slight yearly variations. Please refer to the Ten Thousand Year Calendar for the accurate transition dates for each year.

| Day Master | Ji 己 Earth | Month | Chou 丑 (Ox) |

日元 **Day Master**	月 **Month**
己 *Ji* **Yin Earth**	丑 *Chou* **Ox** **Yin Earth**

For a Ji Earth Day Master born in a Chou (Ox) Month, an Eating God Structure is formed where Xin Metal is revealed as one of the Heavenly Stems.

Where Gui Water is revealed as one of the Heavenly Stems, an Indirect Wealth Structure is formed.

Where Ji Earth is revealed as one of the Heavenly Stems, a Thriving Structure may be formed depending on the condition of the chart.

Should, however, neither Xin Metal, Gui Water nor Ji Earth happen to be revealed within the Heavenly Stems, one should select the BaZi Chart's most prominent Qi attribute at one's discretion.

Day Master Ji 己 Earth	Month Chou 丑 (Ox)

喜用神提要 **Regulating Useful God Reference Guide**

月 Month	用神 Useful God
12th Month 十二月 **Chou** 丑 **(Ox) Month**	丙 *Bing* **Yang Fire** 甲 *Jia* **Yang Wood** 戊 *Wu* **Yang Earth**

Bing Fire, Jia Wood and Wu Earth are the Regulating Useful Gods.

A Ji Earth Day Master born in any of the winter months of Hai (Pig), Zi (Rat) and Chou (Ox) would definitely need Bing Fire to provide 'warmth'. Without Bing Fire, Ji Earth would lack vitality.

Water continues to be strong this month.. This is why Wu Earth is needed to keep excess Water under control.

Where Earth is present in abundance, Jia Wood may be used to 'loosen' it.

Ox

Day Master Ji 己 Earth	Month Chou 丑 (Ox)

6th day of January – 3rd day of February, Gregorian Calendar

A Ji Earth Day Master born in a Chou (Ox) Month is akin to 'wet' or 'icy' Earth.

Given that it is still winter, the sky will be invariably steely and icy, with the ground covered with snow. As such, although the Chou (Ox) Earthly Branch stores excess Earth Qi, it would still be incapable of producing and supporting this Ji Earth Day Master.

Now, although Fire is needed to provide 'warmth' to this Ji Earth Day Master, the capability of Fire to function as a Useful God greatly depends on the availability of Wood, to produce and sustain it. As such, Wood and Fire are the 'arbitrating' Useful Gods for this Day Master.

It is undesirable for this chart to meet with additional Water and Metal Qi. These elements have the capability to counter and weaken Fire, as well as Wood; not to mention adding to the already 'cold' Qi permeating throughout this Day Master's BaZi Chart.

| Day Master | Ji 己 Earth | | Month | Chou 丑 (Ox) |

Commentary

In addition to the preceding narratives on the potential Structures and scenarios resulting from a Ji Earth Day Master born in a Chou (Ox) Month, the following circumstances also play their respective roles in determining the overall strength of this Day Master's BaZi Chart.

Note:

Ox

- Bing Fire and Jia Wood are the primary Useful Gods for a Ji Earth Day Master born in a Hai (Pig), Zi (Rat) or Chou (Ox) Month.

- It is undesirable to have Ren Water and Gui Water from penetrating through the Heavenly Stems.

- Where Ren Water is revealed in the Heavenly Stems or Earthly Branches – while Bing Fire is missing – this Ji Earth Day Master may lack a sense of purpose and direction in life.

- Where Gui Water is revealed in the Heavenly Stems or Earthly Branches – while Companion and Resource Stars are completely missing – a Follow the Wealth Structure is formed in the BaZi Chart. Under such circumstances, this Ji Earth Day Master shall enjoy an extraordinary life of adventure and success.

- Where Wu Earth and Ji Earth penetrate through the Heavenly Stems – together with Jia Wood – this person would enjoy a lot of popularity, fame and recognition. Success comes through his/her connections with other people. Nevertheless, Bing Fire must not be missing from the BaZi Chart. Otherwise non of the positive effects would take place.

- Where Geng Metal penetrates through the Heavenly Stems, Bing Fire and Ding Fire must also be strong, in order that this Ji Earth Day Master to enjoy prolonged prosperity, happiness and fame.

- Regardless of what structure this Ji Earth Day Master may enter into or encounter, Bing Fire must always be present in the chart.

Day Master	Ji 己 Earth	Month	Chou 丑 (Ox)

Additional Attributes

格局 Structural Star	正印 Direct Resource	正官 Direct Officer
用神 Useful God	Bing 丙 Fire	Jia 甲 Wood
Conditions	Where Bing Fire and Jia Wood are both present, this Ji Earth Day Master shall become famous and succeed in his or her career-related pursuits.	
Positive Circumstances	Where Ren Water is present, Wu Earth would be needed to keep it under control.	
Negative Circumstances	Ren Water penetrates through the Heavenly Stems.	

格局 Structural Star	偏財 Indirect Wealth
用神 Useful God	Gui 癸 Water
Conditions	Where a full water structure is formed, Companion Stars are essential for stability of the chart.
Positive Circumstances	Presence of Companion and Resource Stars.
Negative Circumstances	Where Companion and Resource Stars are totally absent, this chart would suffer a obstacles his or her entire life.

Day Master	Ji 己 Earth		Month	Chou 丑 (Ox)

Additional Attributes

格局 Structural Star	劫財 Rob Wealth	比肩 Friend
用神 Useful God	Wu 戊 Earth	Ji 己 Earth
Conditions	Where the Four Graveyard Earthly Branches of Chen (Dragon), Xu (Dog), Chou (Ox) and Wei (Goat) are present form an Earth Structure, Jia Wood is needed to penetrate through the Heavenly Stems.	
Positive Circumstances	Jia Wood in the Heavenly Stems.	
Negative Circumstances	No Jia Wood to penetrate through the Heavenly Stems.	

格局 Structural Star	傷官 Hurting Officer
用神 Useful God	Geng 庚 Metal
Conditions	Where Ding Fire Resource Stars are seen penetrating through the Heavenly Stems, this Ji Earth Day Master shall enjoy prosperity and success throughout his/her life.
Positive Circumstances	Ding Fire rooted and strong.
Negative Circumstances	Absence of Ding Fire.

Bing Fire and Jia Wood are the preferred Useful Gods for a Ji Earth Day Master born in a Hai (Pig), Zi (Rat) or Chou (Ox) Month.

十二月 Twelfth Month

丑 Ox

| Day Master | Ji 己 Earth | Month | Chou 丑 (Ox) |

Summary

- Bing Fire is needed for survival of Ji Earth born in this month.

- A Ji Earth Day Master born in a winter month should use Ding Fire to keep Geng Metal under control.

- Where the full Water formation is formed, additional Companion stars are needed to control the chart's stability. Where this is achieved, this person would enjoy recognition, fame and popularity that is only envied by thousands.

- Where the full Metal formation is formed, Fire Qi is the primary Useful God. Success will only be achieved through much hardship and sacrifice. But great success would eventually be achieved.

- Where Water is present in abundance, Wu Earth the Rob Wealth Star – may be used to keep it under control. In this matter, Ji Earth – a Friend Star – would be of no use.

About Joey Yap

Joey Yap is the Founder and Master Trainer of the Mastery Academy of Chinese Metaphysics, a global organization devoted to the teaching of Feng Shui, BaZi, Mian Xiang and other Chinese Metaphysics subjects. He is also the Chief Consultant of Yap Global Consulting, an international consulting firm specialising in Feng Shui and Chinese Astrology services and audits.

He is the bestselling author of over 25 books, including *Stories and Lessons on Feng Shui, BaZi – The Destiny Code, Mian Xiang – Discover Face Reading, Feng Shui for Homebuyers Series*, and *Pure Feng Shui,* which was released by an international publisher.

He is also the producer of the first comprehensive reference source of Chinese Metaphysics, *The Chinese Metaphysics Compendium*, a compilation of all the essential formulas and applications known and practiced in Chinese Metaphysics today. He has since produced various other reference books and workbooks to aid students in their study and practice of Chinese Metaphysics subjects.

An avid proponent of technology being the way forward in disseminating knowledge of Chinese Metaphysics, Joey has developed, among others, the *BaZi Ming Pan 2.0 Software* and the *Xuan Kong Flying Stars Feng Shui Software*. This passion for fusing the best of modern technology with the best of classical studies lead him to create one of the pioneer online schools for Chinese Metaphysics education, the Mastery Academy E-Learning Centre (www.maelearning.com).

In addition to being a regular guest on various international radio and TV shows, Joey has also written columns for leading newspapers, as well as having contributed articles for various international magazines and publications. He has been featured in many popular publications and media including *Time International*, *Forbes International*, the *International Herald Tribune*, and Bloomberg TV, and was selected as one of Malaysia Tatler's 'Most Influential People in Malaysia' in 2008.

A naturally engaging speaker, Joey has presented to clients like Citibank, HSBC, IBM, Microsoft, Sime Darby, Bloomberg, HP, Samsung, Mah Sing, Nokia, Dijaya, and Standard Chartered.

Joey has also hosted his own TV series, *Discovering Feng Shui with Joey Yap*, and appeared on Malaysia's Astro TV network's *Walking the Dragons with Joey Yap*.

Joey's updates can be followed via Twitter at **www.twitter.com/joeyyap**. A full list of recent events and updates, and more information, can be found at **www.joeyyap.com** and **www.masteryacademy.com**

EDUCATION
The Mastery Academy of Chinese Metaphysics:
the first choice for practitioners and aspiring students of the art and science of Chinese Classical Feng Shui and Astrology.

For thousands of years, Eastern knowledge has been passed from one generation to another through the system of discipleship. A venerated master would accept suitable individuals at a young age as his disciples, and informally through the years, pass on his knowledge and skills to them. His disciples in turn, would take on their own disciples, as a means to perpetuate knowledge or skills.

This system served the purpose of restricting the transfer of knowledge to only worthy honourable individuals and ensuring that outsiders or Westerners would not have access to thousands of years of Eastern knowledge, learning and research.

However, the disciple system has also resulted in Chinese Metaphysics and Classical Studies lacking systematic teaching methods. Knowledge garnered over the years has not been accumulated in a concise, systematic manner, but scattered amongst practitioners, each practicing his/her knowledge, art and science, in isolation.

The disciple system, out of place in today's modern world, endangers the advancement of these classical fields that continue to have great relevance and application today.

At the Mastery Academy of Chinese Metaphysics, our Mission is to bring Eastern Classical knowledge in the fields of metaphysics, Feng Shui and Astrology sciences and the arts to the world. These Classical teachings and knowledge, previously shrouded in secrecy and passed on only through the discipleship system, are adapted into structured learning, which can easily be understood, learnt and mastered. Through modern learning methods, these renowned ancient arts, sciences and practices can be perpetuated while facilitating more extensive application and understanding of these classical subjects.

The Mastery Academy espouses an educational philosophy that draws from the best of the East and West. It is the world's premier educational institution for the study of Chinese Metaphysics Studies offering a wide range and variety of courses, ensuring that students have the opportunity to pursue their preferred field of study and enabling existing practitioners and professionals to gain cross-disciplinary knowledge that complements their current field of practice.

Courses at the Mastery Academy have been carefully designed to ensure a comprehensive yet compact syllabus. The modular nature of the courses enables students to immediately begin to put their knowledge into practice while pursuing continued study of their field and complementary fields. Students thus have the benefit of developing and gaining practical experience in tandem with the expansion and advancement of their theoretical knowledge.

Students can also choose from a variety of study options, from a distance learning program, the Homestudy Series, that enables study at one's own pace or intensive foundation courses and compact lecture-based courses, held in various cities around the world by Joey Yap or our licensed instructors. The Mastery Academy's faculty and make-up is international in nature, thus ensuring that prospective students can attend courses at destinations nearest to their country of origin or with a licensed Mastery Academy instructor in their home country.

The Mastery Academy provides 24x7 support to students through its Online Community, with a variety of tools, documents, forums and e-learning materials to help students stay at the forefront of research in their fields and gain invaluable assistance from peers and mentoring from their instructors.

MASTERY ACADEMY
OF CHINESE METAPHYSICS

www.masteryacademy.com

MALAYSIA
19-3, The Boulevard
Mid Valley City
59200 Kuala Lumpur, Malaysia
Tel　: +603-2284 8080
Fax　: +603-2284 1218
Email : info@masteryacademy.com

SINGAPORE
14, Robinson Road # 13-00
Far East Finance Building
Singapore 048545
Tel　: +65-6494 9147
Email : singapore@masteryacademy.com

Australia, Austria, Canada, China, Croatia, Cyprus, Czech Republic, Denmark, France, Germany, Greece, Hungary, India, Italy, Kazakhstan, Malaysia, Netherlands (Holland), New Zealand, Philippines, Poland, Russian Federation, Singapore, Slovenia, South Africa, Switzerland, Turkey, U.S.A., Ukraine, United Kingdom

Introducing...
The Mastery Academy's E-Learning Center!

The Mastery Academy's goal has always been to share authentic knowledge of Chinese Metaphysics with the whole world.

Nevertheless, we do recognize that distance, time, and hotel and traveling costs – amongst many other factors – could actually hinder people from enrolling for a classroom-based course. But with the advent and amazing advance of IT today, NOT any more!

With this in mind, we have invested heavily in IT, to conceive what is probably the first and only E-Learning Center in the world today that offers a full range of studies in the field of Chinese Metaphysics.

Convenient   Study from Your   Easy Enrollment
                    Own Home

The Mastery Academy's E-Learning Center

Now, armed with your trusty computer or laptop, and Internet access, knowledge of classical Feng Shui, BaZi (Destiny Analysis) and Mian Xiang (Face Reading) are but a literal click away!

Study at your own pace, and interact with your Instructor and fellow students worldwide, from anywhere in the world. With our E-Learning Center, knowledge of Chinese Metaphysics is brought DIRECTLY to you in all its clarity – topic-by-topic, and lesson-by-lesson; with illustrated presentations and comprehensive notes expediting your learning curve!

Your education journey through our E-Learning Center may be done via any of the following approaches:

www.maelearning.com

1. Online Courses

There are 3 Programs available: our Online Feng Shui Program, Online BaZi Program, and Online Mian Xiang Program. Each Program consists of several Levels, with each Level consisting of many Lessons in turn. Each Lesson contains a pre-recorded video session on the topic at hand, accompanied by presentation-slides and graphics as well as downloadable tutorial notes that you can print and file for future reference.

| Video Lecture | Presentation Slide | Downloadable Notes |

2. MA Live!

MA Live!, as its name implies, enables LIVE broadcasts of Joey Yap's courses and seminars – right to your computer screen. Students will not only get to see and hear Joey talk on real-time `live', but also participate and more importantly, TALK to Joey via the MA Live! interface. All the benefits of a live class, minus the hassle of actually having to attend one!

How It Works

Our Live Classes   You at Home

3. Video-On-Demand (VOD)

Get immediate streaming-downloads of the Mastery Academy's wide range of educational DVDs, right on your computer screen. No more shipping costs and waiting time to be incurred!

Instant VOD Online

Choose From Our list   Click "Play" on Your PC
of Available VODs!

Welcome to **www.maelearning.com**; the web portal of our E-Learning Center, and YOUR virtual gateway to Chinese Metaphysics!

Mastery Academy around the world

Canada

United States

Denmark
Czech Republic
Austria
Switzerland
Poland

United Kingdom
Netherlands
France
Italy
Cyprus

Germany
Slovenia
Hungary
Croatia
Greece

Russian
Federation

Ukraine

Turkey

Kazakhstan

India

China

Philippines

Kuala Lumpur
Malaysia

Singapore

Australia

New Zealand

South Africa

YAP GLOBAL CONSULTING

Joey Yap & Yap Global Consulting

Headed by Joey Yap, Yap Global Consulting (YGC) is a leading international consulting firm specializing in Feng Shui, Mian Xiang (Face Reading) and BaZi (Destiny Analysis) consulting services worldwide. Joey - an internationally renowned Master Trainer, Consultant, Speaker and best-selling Author - has dedicated his life to the art and science of Chinese Metaphysics.

YGC has its main offices in Kuala Lumpur and Australia, and draws upon its diverse reservoir of strength from a group of dedicated and experienced consultants based in more than 30 countries, worldwide.

As the pioneer in blending established, classical Chinese Metaphysics techniques with the latest approach in consultation practices, YGC has built its reputation on the principles of professionalism and only the highest standards of service. This allows us to retain the cutting edge in delivering Feng Shui and Destiny consultation services to both corporate and personal clients, in a simple and direct manner, without compromising on quality.

Across Industries: Our Portfolio of Clients

Our diverse portfolio of both corporate and individual clients from all around the world bears testimony to our experience and capabilities.

Virtually every industry imaginable has benefited from our services - ranging from academic and financial institutions, real-estate developers and multinational corporations, to those in the leisure and tourism industry. Our services are also engaged by professionals, prominent business personalities, celebrities, high-profile politicians and people from all walks of life.

YAP GLOBAL CONSULTING

me (Mr./Mrs./Ms.):

ntact Details

l: _____ Fax: _____

bile :_____

mail:_____

hat Type of Consultation Are You Interested In?
☐ Feng Shui ☐ BaZi ☐ Date Selection ☐ Yi Jing

ease tick if applicable:
] Are you a Property Developer looking to engage Yap Global Consulting?

] Are you a Property Investor looking for tailor-made packages to suit your investment requirements?

Please attach your name card here.

Thank you for completing this form. Please fax it back to us at:

Singapore
Tel : +65-6494 9147

Malaysia & the rest of the world
Fax: +603-2284 2213   Tel : +603-2284 1213

---

www.joeyyap.com

Feng Shui Consultations

For Residential Properties
- Initial Land/Property Assessment
- Residential Feng Shui Consultations
- Residential Land Selection
- End-to-End Residential Consultation

For Commercial Properties
- Initial Land/Property Assessment
- Commercial Feng Shui Consultations
- Commercial Land Selection
- End-to-End Commercial Consultation

For Property Developers
- End-to-End Consultation
- Post-Consultation Advisory Services
- Panel Feng Shui Consultant

For Property Investors
- Your Personal Feng Shui Consultant
- Tailor-Made Packages

For Memorial Parks & Burial Sites
- Yin House Feng Shui

BaZi Consultations

Personal Destiny Analysis
- Personal Destiny Analysis for Individuals
- Children's BaZi Analysis
- Family BaZi Analysis

Strategic Analysis for Corporate Organizations
- Corporate BaZi Consultations
- BaZi Analysis for Human Resource Management

Entrepreneurs & Business Owners
- BaZi Analysis for Entrepreneurs

Career Pursuits
- BaZi Career Analysis

Relationships
- Marriage and Compatibility Analysis
- Partnership Analysis

For Everyone
- Annual BaZi Forecast
- Your Personal BaZi Coach**Personal Destiny Analysis**
- Personal Destiny Analysis for Individuals

Date Selection Consultations

- **Marriage Date Selection**
- **Caesarean Birth Date Selection**
- **House-Moving Date Selection**
- **Renovation & Groundbreaking Dates**

- **Signing of Contracts**
- **Official Openings**
- **Product Launches**

Yi Jing Assessment

A Time-Tested, Accurate Science

- With a history predating 4 millennia, the Yi Jing - or Classic of Change - is one of the oldest Chinese texts surviving today. Its purpose as an oracle, in predicting the outcome of things, is based on the variables of Time, Space and Specific Events.

- A Yi Jing Assessment provides specific answers to any specific questions you may have about a specific event or endeavor. This is something that a Destiny Analysis would not be able to give you.

Basically, what a Yi Jing Assessment does is focus on only ONE aspect or item at a particular point in your life, and give you a calculated prediction of the details that will follow suit, if you undertake a particular action. It gives you an insight into a situation, and what course of action to take in order to arrive at a satisfactory outcome at the end of the day.

Please Contact YGC for a personalized Yi Jing Assessment!

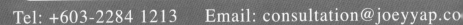

INVITING US TO YOUR CORPORATE EVENTS

Many reputable organizations and institutions have worked closely with YGC to build a synergistic business relationship by engaging our team of consultants, led by Joey Yap, as speakers at their corporate events. Our seminars and short talks are always packed with audiences consisting of clients and associates of multinational and public-listed companies as well as key stakeholders of financial institutions.

We tailor our seminars and talks to suit the anticipated or pertinent group of audience. Be it a department, subsidiary, your clients or even the entire corporation, we aim to fit your requirements in delivering the intended message(s).

Tel: +603-2284 1213   Email: consultation@joeyyap.com

CHINESE METAPHYSICS REFERENCE SERIES

The **Chinese Metaphysics Reference Series** is a collection of reference texts, source material, and educational textbooks to be used as supplementary guides by scholars, students, researchers, teachers and practitioners of Chinese Metaphysics.

These comprehensive and structured books provide fast, easy reference to aid in the study and practice of various Chinese Metaphysics subjects including Feng Shui, BaZi, Yi Jing, Zi Wei, Liu Ren, Ze Ri, Ta Yi, Qi Men and Mian Xiang.

The Chinese Metaphysics Compendium

At over 1,000 pages, the *Chinese Metaphysics Compendium* is a unique one-volume reference book that compiles all the formulas relating to Feng Shui, BaZi (Four Pillars of Destiny), Zi Wei (Purple Star Astrology), Yi Jing (I-Ching), Qi Men (Mystical Doorways), Ze Ri (Date Selection), Mian Xiang (Face Reading) and other sources of Chinese Metaphysics.

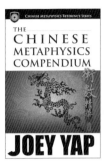

It is presented in the form of easy-to-read tables, diagrams and reference charts, all of which are compiled into one handy book. This first-of-its-kind compendium is presented in both English and the original Chinese, so that none of the meanings and contexts of the technical terminologies are lost.

The only essential and comprehensive reference on Chinese Metaphysics, and an absolute must-have for all students, scholars, and practitioners of Chinese Metaphysics.

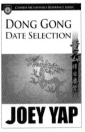

Dong Gong Date Selection

Xuan Kong Da Gua Ten Thousand Year Calendar

Xuan Kong Da Gua Reference Book

The Ten Thousand Year Calendar *(Professional Edition)*

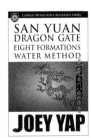

San Yuan Dragon Gate Eight Formations Water Method

Plum Blossoms Divination Reference Book

Qi Men Dun Jia 1080 Charts

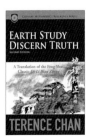

Earth Study Discern Truth Volume Two

Educational Tools & Software

Xuan Kong Flying Stars Feng Shui Software
The Essential Application for Enthusiasts and Professionals

The Xuan Kong Flying Stars Feng Shui Software is a brand-new application by Joey Yap that will assist you in the practice of Xuan Kong Feng Shui with minimum fuss and maximum effectiveness. Superimpose the Flying Stars charts over your house plans (or those of your clients) to clearly demarcate the 9 Palaces. Use it to help you create fast and sophisticated chart drawings and presentations, as well as to assist professional practitioners in the report-writing process before presenting the final reports for your clients. Students can use it to practice their Xuan Kong Feng Shui skills and knowledge, and it can even be used by designers and architects!

Some of the highlights of the software include:
- Natal Flying Stars
- Monthly Flying Stars
- 81 Flying Stars Combinations
- Dual-View Format
- Annual Flying Stars
- Flying Stars Integration
- 24 Mountains

All charts will be are printable and configurable, and can be saved for future editing. Also, you'll be able to export your charts into most image file formats like jpeg, bmp, and gif.

The Xuan Kong Flying Stars Feng Shui Software can make your Feng Shui practice simpler and more effective, garnering you amazing results with less effort!

Mini Feng Shui Compass

This Mini Feng Shui Compass with the accompanying Companion Booklet written by leading Feng Shui and Chinese Astrology Master Trainer Joey Yap is a must-have for any Feng Shui enthusiast.

The Mini Feng Shui Compass is a self-aligning compass that is not only light at 100gms but also built sturdily to ensure it will be convenient to use anywhere. The rings on the Mini Feng Shui Compass are bi-lingual and incorporate the 24 Mountain Rings that is used in your traditional Luo Pan.

The comprehensive booklet included will guide you in applying the 24 Mountain Directions on your Mini Feng Shui Compass effectively and the 8 Mansions Feng Shui to locate the most auspicious locations within your home, office and surroundings. You can also use the Mini Feng Shui Compass when measuring the direction of your property for the purpose of applying Flying Stars Feng Shui.

Educational Tools & Software

BaZi Ming Pan Software Version 2.0
Professional Four Pillars Calculator for Destiny Analysis

The BaZi Ming Pan Version 2.0 Professional Four Pillars Calculator for Destiny Analysis is the most technically advanced software of its kind in the world today. It allows even those without any knowledge of BaZi to generate their own BaZi Charts, and provides virtually every detail required to undertake a comprehensive Destiny Analysis.

This Professional Four Pillars Calculator allows you to even undertake a day-to-day analysis of your Destiny. What's more, all BaZi Charts generated by this software are fully printable and configurable! Designed for both enthusiasts and professional practitioners, this state-of-the-art software blends details with simplicity, and is capable of generating 4 different types of BaZi charts: **BaZi Professional Charts, BaZi Annual Analysis Charts, BaZi Pillar Analysis Charts and BaZi Family Relationship Charts.**

Additional references, configurable to cater to all levels of BaZi knowledge and usage, include:
• Dual Age & Bilingual Option (Western & Chinese) • Na Yin narrations • 12 Life Stages evaluation • Death & Emptiness • Gods & Killings • Special Days • Heavenly Virtue Nobles

This software also comes with a Client Management feature that allows you to save and trace clients' records instantly, navigate effortlessly between BaZi charts, and file your clients' information in an organized manner.

The BaZi Ming Pan Version 2.0 Calculator sets a new standard by combining the best of BaZi and technology.

Joey Yap Feng Shui Template Set

Directions are the cornerstone of any successful Feng Shui audit or application. The **Joey Yap Feng Shui Template Set** is a set of three templates to simplify the process of taking directions and determining locations and positions, whether it's for a building, a house, or an open area such as a plot of land, all with just a floor plan or area map.

The Set comprises 3 basic templates: The Basic Feng Shui Template, 8 Mansions Feng Shui Template, and the Flying Stars Feng Shui Template.

With bi-lingual notations for these directions; both in English and the original Chinese, the **Joey Yap Feng Shui Template Set** comes with its own Booklet that gives simple yet detailed instructions on how to make use of the 3 templates within.

• Easy-to-use, simple, and straightforward
• Small and portable; each template measuring only 5" x 5"
• Additional 8 Mansions and Flying Stars Reference Rings
• Handy companion booklet with usage tips and examples

Accelerate Your Face Reading Skills With
Joey Yap's Face Reading Revealed DVD Series

Mian Xiang, the Chinese art of Face Reading, is an ancient form of physiognomy and entails the use of the face and facial characteristics to evaluate key aspects of a person's life, luck and destiny. In his Face Reading DVDs series, Joey Yap shows you how the facial features reveal a wealth of information about a person's luck, destiny and personality.

Mian Xiang also tell us the talents, quirks and personality of an individual. Do you know that just by looking at a person's face, you can ascertain his or her health, wealth, relationships and career? Let Joey Yap show you how the 12 Palaces can be utilised to reveal a person's inner talents, characteristics and much more.

Each facial feature on the face represents one year in a person's life. Your face is a 100-year map of your life and each position reveals your fortune and destiny at a particular age as well as insights and information about your personality, skills, abilities and destiny.

Using Mian Xiang, you will also be able to plan your life ahead by identifying, for example, the right business partner and knowing the sort of person that you need to avoid. By knowing their characteristics through the facial features, you will be able to gauge their intentions and gain an upper hand in negotiations.

Do you know what moles signify? Do they bring good or bad luck? Do you want to build better relationships with your partner or family members or have your ever wondered why you seem to be always bogged down by trivial problems in your life?

In these highly entertaining DVDs, Joey will help you answer all these questions and more. You will be able to ascertain the underlying meaning of moles, birthmarks or even the type of your hair in Face Reading. Joey will also reveal the guidelines to help you foster better and stronger relationships with your loved ones through Mian Xiang.

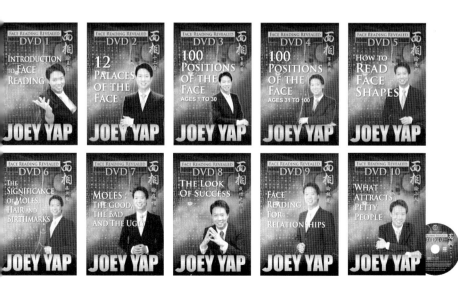

Feng Shui for Homebuyers DVD Series

Best-selling Author, and international Master Trainer and Consultant Joey Yap reveals in these DVD the significant Feng Shui features that every homebuyer should know when evaluating a property.

Joey will guide you on how to customise your home to maximise the Feng Shui potential of you property and gain the full benefit of improving your health, wealth and love life using the 9 Palac Grid. He will show you how to go about applying the classical applications of the Life Gua and House Gua techniques to get attuned to your Sheng Qi (positive energies).

In these DVDs, you will also learn how to identify properties with good Feng Shui features tha will help you promote a fulfilling life and achieve your full potential. Discover how to avoid properties with negative Feng Shui that can bring about detrimental effects to your health, wealth and relationships.

Joey will also elaborate on how to fix the various aspects of your home that may have an impact or the Feng Shui of your property and give pointers on how to tap into the positive energies to suppor your goals.

Discover Feng Shui with Joey Yap (TV Series)

Discover Feng Shui with Joey Yap: Set of 4 DVDs

Informative and entertaining, classical Feng Shui comes alive in *Discover Feng Shu. with Joey Yap!*

Dying to know how you can use Feng Shui to improve your house or office, but simply too busy attend for formal classes?

You have the questions. Now let Joey personally answer them in this 4-set DVD compilation! Learn how to ensure the viability of your residence or workplace, Feng Shui-wise, without having to convert it into a Chinese antiques' shop. Classical Feng Shui is about harnessing the natural power of your environment to improve quality of life. It's a systematic and subtle metaphysical science.

And that's not all. Joey also debunks many a myth about classical Feng Shui, and shares with viewers Face Reading tips as well!

Own the series that national channel 8TV did a re-run of in 2005, today!

Annual Releases

inese Astrology for 2009

information-packed annual guide to the Chinese Astrology for 2009 goes way beyond the ventional 'animal horoscope' book. To begin with, author Joey Yap includes a personalized ook for 2009 based on the individual's BaZi Day Pillar (Jia Zi) and a 12-month micro-ysis for each of the 60 Day Pillars – in addition to the annual outlook for all 12 animal signs the 12-month outlook for each animal sign in 2009. Find out what awaits you in 2009 the four key aspects of Health, Wealth, Career and Relationships…with Joey Yap's **Chinese ology for 2009**!

ng Shui for 2009

imize the Qi of the Year of the Earth Rat for your home and office, with Joey Yap's **Feng Shui 2009** book. Learn how to tap into the positive sectors of the year, and avoid the negative and those with the Annual Afflictions, as well as ascertain how the annual Flying Stars affect property by comparing them against the Eight Mansions (Ba Zhai) for 2009. Flying Stars usiasts will also find this book handy, as it includes the monthly Flying Stars charts for the, accompanied by detailed commentaries on what sectors to use and avoid – to enable you to nize your Academic, Relationships and Wealth Luck in 2009.

ng Shu Diary 2009

anize your professional and personal lives with the **Tong Shu Diary 2009**, with a twist… so allows you to determine the most suitable dates on which you can undertake important ities and endeavors throughout the year! This compact Diary integrates the Chinese Solar Lunar Calendars with the universal lingua franca of the Gregorian Calendar.

ng Shu Monthly Planner 2009

or-made for the Feng Shui or BaZi enthusiast in you, or even professional Chinese aphysics consultants who want a compact planner with useful information incorporated it. In the **Tong Shu Monthly Planner 2009**, you will find the auspicious and inauspicious s for the year marked out for you, alongside the most suitable activities to be undertaken on day. As a bonus, there is also a reference section containing all the monthly Flying Stars ts and Annual Afflictions for 2009.

ng Shu Desktop Calendar 2009

an instant snapshot of the suitable and unsuitable activities for each day of the Year of the th Rat, with the icons displayed on this lightweight Desktop Calendar. Elegantly presenting details of the Chinese Solar Calendar in the form of the standard Gregorian one, the **Tong Desktop Calendar 2009** is perfect for Chinese Metaphysics enthusiasts and practitioners e. Whether it a business launching or meeting, ground breaking ceremony, travel or house-ving that you have in mind, this Calendar is designed to fulfill your information needs.

ng Shu Year Planner 2009

s one-piece Planner presents you all the essential information you need for significant activities ndeavors…with just a quick glance! In a nutshell, it allows you to identify the favorable and avorable days, which will in turn enable you to schedule your year's activities so as to make the st of good days, and avoid the ill-effects brought about by inauspicious ones.

Continue Your Journey with Joey Yap's Books

Walking the Dragons

Walking the Dragons is a guided tour through the classical landform Feng Shui of ancient China, an enchanting collection of deeply-researched yet entertaining essays rich in historical detail.

Compiled in one book for the first time from Joey Yap's Feng Shui Mastery Excursion Series, the book highlights China's extensive, vibrant history with astute observations on the Feng Shui of important sites and places. Learn the landform formations of Yin Houses (tombs and burial places), as well as mountains, temples, castles, and villages.

It demonstrates complex Feng Shui theories and principles in easy-to-understand, entertaining language and is the perfect addition to the bookshelf of a Feng Shui or history lover. Anyone, whether experienc in Feng Shui or new to the practice, will be able to enjoy the insights shared in this book. Complete with gorgec full-colour pictures of all the amazing sights and scenery, it's the next best thing to having been there yourself!

Your Aquarium Here

Your Aquarium Here is a simple, practical, hands-on Feng Shui book that teaches you how to incorporate a Water feature – an aquarium – for optimal Feng Shui benefit, whether for personal relationships, wealth, or career. Designed to be comprehensive yet simple enough for a novice or beginner, *Your Aquarium Here* provides historical and factual information about the role of Water in Feng Shui, and provides a step-by-step guide to installing and using an aquarium.

The book is the first in the **Fengshuilogy Series**, a series of matter-of-fact and useful Feng Shui books designed for the person who wants to do fuss-free Feng Shui. Not everyone who wants to use Feng Shui is an expert or a scholar! This series of books are just the kind you'd want on your bookshelf to gain basic, practical knowledge of the subject. Go ahead and Feng Shui-It-Yourself – *Your Aquarium Here* eliminates all the fuss and bother, but maintains all the fun and excitement, of authentic Feng Shui application!

The Art of Date Selection: Personal Date Selection

In today's modern world, it is not good enough to just do things effectively – we need to do them efficiently, as well. From the signing of business contracts and moving into a new home, to launching a product or even tying the knot; everything has to move, and move very quickly too. There is a premium on Time, where mistakes can indeed be costly.

The notion of doing the Right Thing, at the Right Time and in the Right Place is the very backbone of Date Selection. Because by selecting a suitable date specially tailored to a specific activity or endeavor, we infuse it with the most positive energies prevalent in our environment during that particular point in time; and that could well make the difference between `make-and-break'! With the *Art of Date Selection: Personal Date Selection*, learn simple, practical methods you can employ to select not just go dates, but personalized good dates. Whether it's a personal activity such as a marriage or professional endeavor such launching a business, signing a contract or even acquiring assets, this book will show you how to pick the good da and tailor them to suit the activity in question, as well as avoid the negative ones too!

The Art of Date Selection: Feng Shui Date Selection

Date Selection is the Art of selecting the most suitable date, where the energies present on the day support the specific activities or endeavors we choose to undertake on that day. Feng Shui is the Chinese Metaphysical study of the Physiognomy of the Land – landforms and the Qi they produce, circulate and conduct. Hence, anything that exists on this Earth is invariably subject to the laws of Feng Shui. So what do we get when Date Selection and Feng Shui converge?

Feng Shui Date Selection, of course! Say you wish to renovate your home, or maybe buy or rent one. Or perhaps, you're a developer, and wish to know WHEN is the best date possible to commence construction works on your project. In any case – and all cases – you certainly wish to ensure that your endeavors are well supported by the positive energies present on a good day, won't you? And this is where Date Selection supplements the practice of Feng Shui. At the end of the day, it's all about making the most of what's good, and minimizing what's bad.

(Available Soon)

Continue Your Journey with Joey Yap's Books

Feng Shui For Homebuyers - Exterior

Best selling Author and international Feng Shui Consultant, Joey Yap, will guide you on the various important features in your external environment that have a bearing on the Feng Shui of your home. For homeowners, those looking to build their own home or even investors who are looking to apply Feng Shui to their homes, this book provides valuable information from the classical Feng Shui theories and applications.

This book will assist you in screening and eliminating unsuitable options with negative FSQ (Feng Shui Quotient) should you acquire your own land or if you are purchasing a newly built home. It will also help you in determining which plot of land to select and which to avoid when purchasing an empty parcel of land.

Feng Shui for Homebuyers - Interior

A book every homeowner or potential house buyer should have. The Feng Shui for Homebuyers (Interior) is an informative reference book and invaluable guide written by best selling Author and international Feng Shui Consultant, Joey Yap.

This book provides answers to the important questions of what really does matter when looking at the internal Feng Shui of a home or office. It teaches you how to analyze your home or office floor plans and how to improve their Feng Shui. It will answer all your questions about the positive and negative flow of Qi within your home and ways to utilize them to your maximum benefit.

Providing you with a guide to calculating your Life Gua and House Gua to fine-tune your Feng Shui within your property, Joey Yap focuses on practical, easily applicable ideas on what you can implement internally in a property.

Feng Shui for Apartment Buyers - Home Owners

Finding a good apartment or condominium is never an easy task but who do you ensure that is also has good Feng Shui? And how exactly do you apply Feng Shui to an apartment or condominium or high-rise residence?

These questions and more are answered by renowned Feng Shui Consultant and Master Trainer Joey Yap in **Feng Shui for Apartment Buyers - Home Owners**. Joey answers the key questions about Feng Shui and apartments, then guides you through the bare basics like taking a direction and super-imposing a Flying Stars chart onto a floor plan. Joey also walks you through the process of finding an apartment with favorable Feng Shui, sharing with you some of the key methods and techniques that are employed by professional Feng Shui consultants in assesing apartment Feng Shui.

In his trademark straight-to-the-point manner, Joey shares with you the Feng Shui do's and dont's when it comes to finding an apartment with favorable Feng Shui and which is conducive for home living.

The Ten Thousand Year Calendar

The Ten Thousand Year Calendar or 萬年曆 Wan Nian Li is a regular reference book and an invaluable tool used by masters, practitioners and students of Feng Shui, BaZi (Four Pillars of Destiny), Chinese Zi Wei Dou Shu Astrology (Purple Star), Yi Jing (I-Ching) and Date Selection specialists.

JOEY YAP's *Ten Thousand Year Calendar* provides the Gregorian (Western) dates converted into both the Chinese Solar and Lunar calendar in both the English and Chinese language.

It also includes a comprehensive set of key Feng Shui and Chinese Astrology charts and references, including Xuan Kong Nine Palace Flying Star Charts, Monthly and Daily Flying Stars, Water Dragon Formulas Reference Charts, Zi Wei Dou Shu (Purple Star) Astrology Reference Charts, BaZi (Four Pillars of Destiny) Heavenly Stems, Earthly Branches and all other related reference tables for Chinese Metaphysical Studies.

Continue Your Journey with Joey Yap's Books

Stories and Lessons on Feng Shui (English & Chinese versions)

Stories and Lessons on Feng Shui is a compilation of essays and stories written by leading Feng Shui and Chinese Astrology trainer and consultant Joey Yap about Feng Shui and Chinese Astrology.

In this heart-warming collection of easy to read stories, find out why it's a myth that you should never have Water on the right hand side of your house, the truth behind the infamous 'love' and 'wealth' corners and that the sudden death of a pet fish is really NOT due to bad luck!

More Stories and Lessons on Feng Shui

Finally, the long-awaited sequel to *Stories & Lessons on Feng Shui*!

If you've read the best-selling Stories & Lessons on Feng Shui, you won't want to miss this book. And even if you haven't read *Stories & Lessons on Feng Shui*, there's always a time to rev your Feng Shui engine up.

The time is NOW.

And the book? *More Stories & Lessons on Feng Shui* – the 2nd compilation of the most popular articles and columns penned by Joey Yap; **specially featured in national and international publications, magazines and newspapers.**

All in all, *More Stories & Lessons on Feng Shui* is a delightful chronicle of Joey's articles, thoughts and vast experience - as a professional Feng Shui consultant and instructor - that have been purposely refined, edited and expanded upon to make for a light-hearted, interesting yet educational read. And with Feng Shui, BaZi, Mian Xiang and Yi Jing all thrown into this one dish, there's something for everyone...so all you need to serve or accompany *More Stories & Lessons on Feng Shui* with is your favorite cup of tea or coffee!

Even More Stories and Lessons on Feng Shui

In this third release in the Stories and Lessons series, Joey Yap continues his exploration on the study and practice of Feng Shui in the modern age through a series of essays and personal anecdotes. Debunking superstition, offering simple and understandable "Feng Shui-It-Yourself" tips, and expounding on the history and origins of classical Feng Shui, Joey takes readers on a journey that is always refreshing and exciting.

Besides 'behind-the-scenes' revelations of actual Feng Shui audits, there are also chapters on how beginners can easily and accurately incorporate Feng Shui practice into their lives, as well as travel articles that offer proof that when it comes to Feng Shui, the Qi literally knows no boundaries.

In his trademark lucid and forthright style, Joey covers themes and topics that will strike a chord with all readers who have an interest in Feng Shui.

Mian Xiang - Discover Face Reading

Need to identify a suitable business partner? How about understanding your staff or superiors better? Or even choosing a suitable spouse? These mind boggling questions can be answered in Joey Yap's introductory book to Face Reading titled *Mian Xiang – Discover Face Reading*. This book will help you discover the hidden secrets in a person's face.

Mian Xiang – Discover Face Reading is comprehensive book on all areas of Face Reading, covering some of the most important facial features, including the forehead, mouth, ears and even the philtrum above your lips. This book will help you analyse not just your Destiny but help you achieve your full potential and achieve life fulfillment.

Continue Your Journey with Joey Yap's Books

BaZi - The Destiny Code (English & Chinese versions)

Leading Chinese Astrology Master Trainer Joey Yap makes it easy to learn how to unlock your Destiny through your BaZi with this book. BaZi or Four Pillars of Destiny is an ancient Chinese science which enables individuals to understand their personality, hidden talents and abilities as well as their luck cycle, simply by examining the information contained within their birth data. The Destiny Code is the first book that shows readers how to plot and interpret their own Destiny charts and lays the foundation for more in-depth BaZi studies. Written in a lively entertaining style, the Destiny Code makes BaZi accessible to the layperson. Within 10 chapters, understand and appreciate more about this astoundingly accurate ancient Chinese Metaphysical science.

BaZi - The Destiny Code Revealed

In this follow up to Joey Yap's best-selling The Destiny Code, delve deeper into your own Destiny chart through an understanding of the key elemental relationships that affect the Heavenly Stems and Earthly Branches. Find out how Combinations, Clash, Harm, Destructions and Punishments bring new dimension to a BaZi chart. Complemented by extensive real-life examples, The Destiny Code Revealed takes you to the next level of BaZi, showing you how to unlock the Codes of Destiny and to take decisive action at the right time, and capitalise on the opportunities in life.

Xuan Kong: Flying Stars Feng Shui

Xuan Kong Flying Stars Feng Shui is an essential introductory book to the subject of Xuan Kong Fei Xing, a well-known and popular system of Feng Shui, written by International Feng Shui Master Trainer Joey Yap.

In his down-to-earth, entertaining and easy to read style, Joey Yap takes you through the essential basics of Classical Feng Shui, and the key concepts of Xuan Kong Fei Xing (Flying Stars). Learn how to fly the stars, plot a Flying Star chart for your home or office and interpret the stars and star combinations. Find out how to utilise the favourable areas of your home or office for maximum benefit and learn 'tricks of the trade' and 'trade secrets' used by Feng Shui practitioners to enhance and maximise Qi in your home or office.

An essential integral introduction to the subject of Classical Feng Shui and the Flying Stars System of Feng Shui!

Xuan Kong Flying Stars: Structures and Combinations

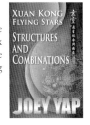

Delve deeper into Flying Stars through a greater understanding of the 81 Combinations and the influence of the Annual and Monthly Stars on the Base, Sitting and Facing Stars in this 2nd book in the Xuan Kong Feng Shui series. Learn how Structures like the Combination of 10, Up the Mountain and Down the River, Pearl and Parent String Structures are used to interpret a Flying Star chart.

(Available Soon)

Xuan Kong Flying Stars: Advanced Techniques

Take your knowledge of Xuan Kong Flying Stars to a higher level and learn how to apply complex techniques and advanced formulas such as Castle Gate Technique, Seven Star Robbery Formation, Advancing the Dragon Formation and Replacement Star technique amongst others. Joey Yap also shows you how to use the Life Palace technique to combine Gua Numbers with Flying Star numbers and utilise the predictive facets of Flying Stars Feng Shui.

(Available Soon)

Elevate Your Feng Shui Skills With Joey Yap's Home Study Course And Educational DVDs

Xuan Kong Vol.1
An Advanced Feng Shui Home Study Course

Learn the Xuan Kong Flying Star Feng Shui system in just 20 lessons! Joey Yap's specialised notes and course work have been written to enable distance learning without compromising on the breadth or quality of the syllabus. Learn at your own pace with the same material students in a live class would use. The most comprehensive distance learning course on Xuan Kong Flying Star Feng Shui in the market. Xuan Kong Flying Star Vol.1 comes complete with a special binder for all your course notes.

Feng Shui for Period 8 - (DVD)

Don't miss the Feng Shui Event of the next 20 years! Catch Joey Yap LIVE and find out just what Period 8 is all about. This DVD boxed set zips you through the fundamentals of Feng Shui and the impact of this important change in the Feng Shui calendar. Joey's entertaining, conversational style walks you through the key changes that Period 8 will bring and how to tap into Wealth Qi and Good Feng Shui for the next 20 years.

Xuan Kong Flying Stars Beginners Workshop - (DVD)

Take a front row seat in Joey Yap's Xuan Kong Flying Stars workshop with this unique LIVE RECORDING of Joey Yap's Xuan Kong Flying Stars Feng Shui workshop, attended by over 500 people. This DVD program provides an effective and quick introduction of Xuan Kong Feng Shui essentials for those who are just starting out in their study of classical Feng Shui. Learn to plot your own Flying Star chart in just 3 hours. Learn 'trade secret' methods, remedies and cures for Flying Stars Feng Shui. This boxed set contains 3 DVDs and 1 workbook with notes and charts for reference.

BaZi Four Pillars of Destiny Beginners Workshop - (DVD)

Ever wondered what Destiny has in store for you? Or curious to know how you can learn more about your personality and inner talents? BaZi or Four Pillars of Destiny is an ancient Chinese science that enables us to understand a person's hidden talent, inner potential, personality, health and wealth luck from just their birth data. This specially compiled DVD set of Joey Yap's BaZi Beginners Workshop provides a thorough and comprehensive introduction to BaZi. Learn how to read your own chart and understand your own luck cycle. This boxed set contains 3 DVDs and 1 workbook with notes and reference charts.

Interested in learning MORE about Feng Shui? Advance Your Feng Shui Knowledge with the Mastery Academy Courses.

Feng Shui Mastery Series™
LIVE COURSES (MODULES ONE TO FOUR)

Feng Shui Mastery – Module One
Beginners Course

Designed for students seeking an entry-level intensive program into the study of Feng Shui , Module One is an intensive foundation course that aims not only to provide you with an introduction to Feng Shui theories and formulas and equip you with the skills and judgments to begin practicing and conduct simple Feng Shui audits upon successful completion of the course. Learn all about Forms, Eight Mansions Feng Shui and Flying Star Feng Shui in just one day with a unique, structured learning program that makes learning Feng Shui quick and easy!

Feng Shui Mastery – Module Two
Practitioners Course

Building on the knowledge and foundation in classical Feng Shui theory garnered in M1, M2 provides a more advanced and in-depth understanding of Eight Mansions, Xuan Kong Flying Star and San He and introduces students to theories that are found only in the classical Chinese Feng Shui texts. This 3-Day Intensive course hones analytical and judgment skills, refines Luo Pan (Chinese Feng Shui compass) skills and reveals 'trade secret' remedies. Module Two covers advanced Forms Analysis, San He's Five Ghost Carry Treasure formula, Advanced Eight Mansions and Xuan Kong Flying Stars and equips you with the skills needed to undertake audits and consultations for residences and offices.

Feng Shui Mastery – Module Three
Advanced Practitioners Course

Module Three is designed for Professional Feng Shui Practitioners. Learn advanced topics in Feng Shui and take your skills to a cutting edge level. Be equipped with the knowledge, techniques and confidence to conduct large scale audits (like estate and resort planning). Learn how to apply different systems appropriately to remedy situations or cases deemed inauspicious by one system and reconcile conflicts in different systems of Feng Shui. Gain advanced knowledge of San He (Three Harmony) systems and San Yuan (Three Cycles) systems, advanced Luan Tou (Forms Feng Shui) and specialist Water Formulas.

Feng Shui Mastery – Module Four
Master Course

The graduating course of the Feng Shui Mastery (FSM) Series, this course takes the advanced practitioner to the Master level. Power packed M4 trains students to 'walk the mountains' and identify superior landform, superior grade structures and make qualitative evaluations of landform, structures, Water and Qi and covers advanced and exclusive topics of San He, San Yuan, Xuan Kong, Ba Zhai, Luan Tou (Advanced Forms and Water Formula) Feng Shui. Master Internal, External and Luan Tou (Landform) Feng Shui methodologies to apply Feng Shui at every level and undertake consultations of every scale and magnitude, from houses and apartments to housing estates, townships, shopping malls and commercial districts.

BaZi Mastery Series™
LIVE COURSES (MODULES ONE TO FOUR)

BaZi Mastery – Module One
Intensive Foundation Course

This Intensive One Day Foundation Course provides an introduction to the principles and fundamentals of BaZi (Four Pillars of Destiny) and Destiny Analysis methods such as Ten Gods, Useful God and Strength of Qi. Learn how to plot a BaZi chart and interpret your Destiny and your potential. Master BaZi and learn to capitalize on your strengths, minimize risks and downturns and take charge of your Destiny.

BaZi Mastery – Module Two
Practical BaZi Applications

BaZi Module Two teaches students advanced BaZi analysis techniques and specific analysis methods for relationship luck, health evaluation, wealth potential and career potential. Students will learn to identify BaZi chart structures, sophisticated methods for applying the Ten Gods, and how to read Auxiliary Stars. Students who have completed Module Two will be able to conduct professional BaZi readings.

BaZi Mastery – Module Three
Advanced Practitioners Program

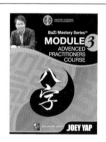

Designed for the BaZi practitioner, learn how to read complex cases and unique events in BaZi charts and perform Big and Small assessments. Discover how to analyze personalities and evaluate talents precisely, as well as special formulas and classical methodologies for BaZi from classics such as Di Tian Sui and Qiong Tong Bao Jian.

BaZi Mastery – Module Four
Master Course in BaZi

The graduating course of the BaZi Mastery Series, this course takes the advanced practitioner to the Masters' level. BaZi M4 focuses on specialized techniques of BaZi reading, unique special structures and advance methods from ancient classical texts. This program includes techniques on date selection and ancient methodologies from the Qiong Tong Bao Jian and Yuan Hai Zi Ping classics.

Xuan Kong Mastery – Module One
Advanced Foundation Program

This course is for the experienced Feng Shui professionals who wish to expand their knowledge and skills in the Xuan Kong system of Feng Shui, covering important foundation methods and techniques from the Wu Chang and Guang Dong lineages of Xuan Kong Feng Shui.

Xuan Kong Mastery – Module Two A
Advanced Xuan Kong Methodologies

Designed for Feng Shui practitioners seeking to specialise in the Xuan Kong system, this program focuses on methods of application and Joey Yap's unique Life Palace and Shifting Palace Methods, as well as methods and techniques from the Wu Chang lineage.

Xuan Kong Mastery – Module Two B
Purple White

Explore in detail and in great depth the star combinations in Xuan Kong. Learn how each different combination reacts or responds in different palaces, under different environmental circumstances and to whom in the property. Learn methods, theories and techniques extracted from ancient classics such as Xuan Kong Mi Zhi, Xuan Kong Fu, Fei Xing Fu and Zi Bai Jue.

Xuan Kong Mastery – Module Three
Advanced Xuan Kong Da Gua

This intensive course focuses solely on the Xuan Kong Da Gua system covering the theories, techniques and methods of application of this unique 64-Hexagram based system of Xuan Kong including Xuan Kong Da Gua for landform analysis.

Walk the Mountains! Learn Feng Shui in a Practical and Hands-on Program

Feng Shui Mastery Excursion Series™ : CHINA

Learn landform (Luan Tou) Feng Shui by walking the mountains and chasing the Dragon's vein in China. This Program takes the students in a study tour to examine notable Feng Shui landmarks, mountains, hills, valleys, ancient palaces, famous mansions, houses and tombs in China. The Excursion is a 'practical' hands-on course where students are shown to perform readings using the formulas they've learnt and to recognize and read Feng Shui Landform (Luan Tou) formations.

Read about China Excursion here:
http://www.masteryacademy.com/Education/schoolfengshui/fengshuimasteryexcursion.asp

Mian Xiang Mastery Series™
LIVE COURSES (MODULES ONE AND TWO)

Mian Xiang Mastery – Module One
Basic Face Reading

A person's face is their fortune – learn more about the ancient Chinese art of Face Reading. In just one day, be equipped with techniques and skills to read a person's face and ascertain their character, luck, wealth and relationship luck.

Mian Xiang Mastery – Module Two
Practical Face Reading

Mian Xiang Module Two covers face reading techniques extracted from the ancient classics Shen Xiang Quan Pian and Shen Xiang Tie Guan Dau. Gain a greater depth and understanding of Mian Xiang and learn to recognize key structures and characteristics in a person's face.

Yi Jing Mastery Series™
LIVE COURSES (MODULES ONE AND TWO)

Yi Jing Mastery – Module One
Traditional Yi Jing

'Yi', relates to change. Change is the only constant in life and the universe, without exception to this rule. The Yi Jing is hence popularly referred to as the Book or Classic of Change. Discoursed in the language of Yin and Yang, the Yi Jing is one of the oldest Chinese classical texts surviving today. With Traditional Yi Jing, learnn how this Classic is used to divine the outcomes of virtually every facet of life; from your relationships to seeking an answer to the issues you may face in your daily life.

Yi Jing Mastery – Module Two
Plum Blossom Numerology

Shao Yong, widely regarded as one of the greatest scholars of the Sung Dynasty, developed Mei Hua Yi Shu (Plum Blossom Numerology) as a more advanced means for divination purpose using the Yi Jing. In Plum Blossom Numerology, the results of a hexagram are interpreted by referring to the Gua meanings, where the interaction and relationship between the five elements, stems, branches and time are equally taken into consideration. This divination method, properly applied, allows us to make proper decisions whenever we find ourselves in a predicament.

Ze Ri Mastery Series™
LIVE COURSES (MODULES ONE AND TWO)

Ze Ri Mastery Series Module 1
Personal and Feng Shui Date Selection

The Mastery Academy's Date Selection Mastery Series Module 1 is specifically structured to provide novice students with an exciting introduction to the Art of Date Selection. Learn the rudiments and tenets of this intriguing metaphysical science. What makes a good date, and what makes a bad date? What dates are suitable for which activities, and what dates simply aren't? And of course, the mother of all questions: WHY aren't all dates created equal. All in only one Module – Module 1!

Ze Ri Mastery Series Module 2
Xuan Kong Da Gua Date Selection

In Module 2, discover advanced Date Selection techniques that will take your knowledge of this Art to a level equivalent to that of a professional's! This is the Module where Date Selection infuses knowledge of the ancient metaphysical science of Feng Shui and BaZi (Chinese Astrology, or Four Pillars of Destiny). Feng Shui, as a means of maximizing Human Luck (i.e. our luck on Earth), is often quoted as the cure to BaZi, which allows us to decipher our Heaven (i.e. inherent) Luck. And one of the most potent ways of making the most of what life has to offer us is to understand our Destiny, know how we can use the natural energies of our environment for our environments and MOST importantly, WHEN we should use these energies and for WHAT endeavors!

You will learn specific methods on how to select suitable dates, tailored to specific activities and events. More importantly, you will also be taught how to suit dates to a person's BaZi (Chinese Astrology, or Four Pillars of Destiny), in order to maximize his or her strengths, and allow this person to surmount any challenges that lie in wait. Add in the factor of `place', and you would have satisfied the notion of `doing the right thing, at the right time and in the right place'! A basic knowledge of BaZi and Feng Shui will come in handy in this Module, although these are not pre-requisites to successfully undergo Module 2.

Feng Shui for Life

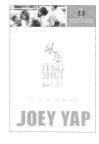

Feng Shui for life is a 5-day course designed for the Feng Shui beginner to learn how to apply practical Feng Shui in day-to-day living. It is a culmination of powerful tools and techniques that allows you to gain quick proficiency in Classical Feng Shui. Discover quick tips on analysing your own BaZi, how to apply Feng Shui solutions for your own home, how to select auspicious dates for important activities, as well as simple and useful Face Reading techniques and practical Water Formulas. This is a complete beginner's course that is suitable for anyone with an interest in applying practical, real-world Feng Shui for life! Enhance every aspect of your life – your health, wealth, and relationships – using these easy-to-apply Classical Feng Shui methods.

Mastery Academy courses are conducted around the world. Find out when will Joey Yap be in your area by visiting **www.masteryacademy.com** or call our office at **+603-2284 8080**.